European Practice Library

IMMIGRATION LAW AND BUSINESS IN EUROPE

Edited by
Paul Gulbenkian
and
Ted Badoux

Business Editors
Lionel Harris
and
Franz Tepper

EEIG
European Immigration
Lawyers Group

Chancery Law Publishing
A Division of John Wiley & Sons,
London, New York, Chichester, Brisbane, Toronto, Singapore.

Published in Great Britain by
Chancery Law Publishing Ltd
Baffins Lane
Chichester PO19 1UD

Published in North America by
John Wiley & Sons Inc.
7222 Commerce Center Drive
Colorado Springs, CO 80919
USA

Typeset by
Vision Typesetting,
Manchester
Printed and bound in Great Britain by
Ipswich Book Company Ltd

ISBN 0471 94048 8

A copy of the CIP entry for this book is available
from the British Library.

Library of Congress Cataloging-in-Publication Data

Immigration law and business in Europe / edited by Paul Gulbenkian
[and] EEIG, European Immigration Lawyers Group.
p. cm. – (European practice library)
Includes index.
ISBN 0-471-94048-8 (cloth)
1. Emigration and immigration law – Europe. 2. Domicile – Europe
3. Alien labor – Legal status, laws, etc. – Europe. 4. Emigration and
immigration law – European Economic Community countries. 5. Freedom
of movement – European Economic Community countries. I. Gulbenkian,
Paul. II. European Immigration Lawyers Group. III. Series.
KJC6044.I46   1993
342.4′082.0282–dc20   93–10859 CIP

Contents

CONTENTS

CONTENTS

CONTENTS

Preface

Imigration Law and Business in Europe is a publication of the European Immigration Lawyers Group (EILG). The Group is a network of 13 European law firms represented in each EC country and Sweden who specialise in matters of national and EC immigration law. The aims of the Group are:

(i)   to work together in obtaining work permits for corporate employees within the EC, including employees moving from one Member State to another;

(ii) to find means of transferring residence from countries of second choice to countries of first choice within the EC nationality rules; and

(iii) to provide a "one stop" comprehensive European Immigration Service to non-EC nationals.

Immigration Law and Business in Europe is published to provide practical and basic information on immigration rules and policies within the European Community. As from 1992 it has become clear that there will be those who may enjoy the rights of an "open European society" and those who may not. The book provides a helpful guide for individuals and corporate entities interested in moving themselves or their employees to or settling in EC countries. It will help them to find out whether they may belong to a privileged European category, which privileges they might enjoy and which conditions should be met to obtain residence and/or a work permit in each of the Member States of the European Community. Others, without obvious privileges, may find in the following pages that they have certain rights in accordance with special EC Regulations or that national policies or rules may offer better opportunities in one particular Member State than in another.

This is not a "do it yourself" book. But for those faced with important questions as to where in Europe to do or start business, where in Europe to study, to work, to invest or enjoy a pension, the book offers help in understanding the European situation and the options available in each of the Member States.

It cannot be emphasised enough that in all European countries immigration laws and policies are very complex and that each case is considered and decided on its own merits. It is, therefore, essential, in addition to consulting this work, to obtain expert advice and guidance.

The countries participating in this work are listed in alphabetical order. Thanks are due to the authors of the various chapters and to everyone who gave encouragement and support for the preparation of this book. Although contributors have all followed a consistent pattern they have each been given latitude to bring in or emphasise aspects they consider especially important in their jurisdiction. The law is stated as at 28 February 1993.

The law firms participating in the European Immigration Lawyers Group are specified overleaf:

Belgium

Mackelbert, de Salle,
Antoine Bricart,
Levert & Englebert
Avenue Clémentine 3
1060 Brussels

Tel: (32)(2)5345098
Fax: (32)(2)5345402

Denmark

Norsker & Jacoby
Kvaesthusgade 3
DK 1251 Copenhagen K

Tel: (45)33110885
Fax: (45)33937530

France

Pierre Pascal Bruneau & Associes
22 Place Du General Catroux
75017 Paris

Tel; (33)(1)47669994
Fax: (33)(1)47668307

Germany

Brandi Droge Piltz & Heuer
Hochstrasse 19
W-4830 Gutersloh

Tel: (49)(5241)58886
Fax: (49)(5241)58881

Greece

Vgenopoulos & Partners
15 Kolonaki Square
Athens 106 73

Tel: (30)7221 832/7217 803
Fax: (30)7231 462

Ireland

Eugene F Collins
61 Fitzwilliam Square
Dublin 2

Tel: (353)(1)785766
Fax: (353)(1)618906

Italy

Umberto Astoli
20122 Milano
C.so Porta Vittoria, 14

Tel: (39)(2)55183100
Fax: (39)(2)5466743

Luxembourg

Faltz Association
PO Box 1147
L-1011 Luxembourg

Tel: (35)(2)485050
Fax: (35)(2)481385

Netherlands

Everaert Advokaten
Keizersgracht 410
1016 GC Amsterdam

Tel: (31)(20)6271181
Fax: (31)(20)6273231

Portugal

Jose Alves Pereira and Associates
Ave. de Berna No. 4-1 Dto
1000 Lisbon

Tel: (35)(1)7938890
Fax: (35)(1)7938889

Spain

Gomez-Acebo & Pombo
Castellana, 164
28046 Madrid

Tel: (34)(1)5829100
Fax. (34)(1)3453679
          5829114

Sweden

Skarholmens Advokatbyra
Box 237
12725 Skarholmen
Stockholm

Tel: (46)(8)7401850
Fax: (46)(8)7401717

United Kingdom

Gulbenkian Harris
Andonian
181 Kensington High Street
London W8 6SH

Tel: (44)(71)9371542
Fax: (44)(71)9382059

EC Nationals: an European Overview

Chapter 1
EC Nationals: an European Overview*

After the Second World War a political movement emerged in Europe which **1.1**
aspired to create strongly organised political and economic relations between
the European nations. In the 1950s the later Benelux countries, France,
Germany and Italy founded three European Communities for the gradual
integration of their economies. In 1965 these three Communities were
integrated into the European Community (EC) by the Treaty of Rome.

In 1986 the EC Member States signed the Single European Act setting out
the principles and a time schedule for further political and economic
integration, including the achievement of a single market by 1 January
1993.

At the Summit of Maastricht in December 1991 the EC Member States **1.2**
agreed on a Monetary and Political Union with the exception of the United
Kingdom. A Common European Currency (ECU) will be introduced
between 1996 and 1999. A Central European Bank will be founded not later
than 1 July 1998. Defence, foreign policy and labour conditions will be
integrated on the basis of inter-governmental co-operation.

One of the aims of the European Community is to establish a common **1.3**
market. This should be achieved, among other things, by the abolition
between Member States of obstacles to the freedom of movement for persons,
services and capital. The EEC Treaty warrants the freedom of nationals of
Member States to pursue economic activities in other Member States. The
EEC Treaty provides for the free movement of workers in Articles 48 to 51, the
right of establishment in Articles 52 to 58 and the right to receive and be the
recipient of services in Articles 59 to 66. Pursuant to Article 7 all EC nationals
have the right to enjoy these freedoms without any discrimination on the basis
of nationality. EC nationals are defined as people who hold valid passports as
citizens of any individual EC Member State.

The implementation of these freedoms is governed by Regulations and **1.4**
Directives which are binding upon the Member States and have priority over
national law. The EC provisions with regard to the rights of EC nationals are
to be inforced by the national courts on the basis of this principle of direct
applicability.

---

* Parts of this text are also included in an article on the Netherlands by Ted Badoux in: "Immigration
and Nationality Law" to be published by Kluwer Academic Publishers in an edition of the Center for
International Legal Studies in Salzburg, Austria.

The European Court of Justice in Luxembourg plays an important part in the development of Community law, especially through interpretative rulings. In the field of immigration law its jurisprudence, which is a binding upon the Member States as well, has had a major impact on issues such as education, employment, family life and public policy.

1.5   In 1992 the Member States of the EC were: Belgium, Denmark, France, Germany, Greece, Ireland, Italy, Luxembourg, The Netherlands, Portugal, Spain and the United Kingdom. Austria and Sweden may join the European Community as of January 1995. By the end of 1991 Hungary, Poland and Czechoslovakia entered into Agreements of Association with the European Community. Turkey, Morocco, Tunisia, Malta and Cyprus have become associated with the EC in the 1960s and 1970s. Recent jurisprudence of the European Court of Justice – the case of Mr Sevince from Turkey, the case of Ms Kziber from Morocco and the case of Mr Kus from Turkey – shows that the rules in these agreements may be very important for residence, the right to work and the social benefits of workers from associated countries.

1.6   Apart from these agreements of association/co-operation the European Community upholds extensive trade relations with countries and organisations of countries throughout the world. In October 1991 the European Community agreed with the European Free Trade Area (EFTA) countries (Austria, Finland, Iceland, Liechtenstein, Norway, Sweden and Switzerland) to create a European Economic Area (European Economic Area Agreement (EEAA)). It was intended, that the nationals of the EFTA-countries would enjoy the EC rights of free circulation for employment and establishment as of 1 January 1993. However, the necessary national ratification procedures have not been completed at the time of writing and the Swiss have voted themselves out of the EEAA by national referendum.

1. **Rights of free movement**

1.7   European nationals who migrate for economic purposes from one State in the Community to another, take a privileged position. They may have found work either in employment or in self-employment. They may have come to seek employment or self-employment or they may wish to provide or receive services.

(i) **Employment**

1.8   The rights of free movement of workers are set out in Articles 48–51 of the EEC Treaty. According to Article 48, paragraph 3 of the EEC Treaty, the free movement of workers entails the right:
- to accept actual offers of employment;
- to move freely within EC territory for this purpose;
- to stay in the territory of an EC country for the purposes of employment;
- to remain there after having been employed.

These provisions have been implemented by Regulation 1612/68, which **1.9** deals with non-discrimination and the worker's family, by Directive 68/360, which grants workers and their families the right of entry and residence, and by Regulation 1251/70, which gives workers and their families the right to remain in a Member State after retirement or permanent incapacity.

EC nationals seeking employment have the right to enter and seek employment for three months as long as they do not attempt to live on welfare. They are not obliged to show sufficient means upon entry. Border officials are not authorised to question job-seeking EC nationals on sufficient means. The three months term is not very strict it would seem; 6 months may be a reasonable term also and even this term may be overstepped if it is demonstrated that efforts to find employment are still being made and that the prospects of success are realistic.

EC nationals seeking employment, must report to the local authorities in **1.10** charge of immigration. These authorities in their turn are obliged to refer job-seeking EC nationals to the domestic bodies for employment-finding. EC nationals are entitled to the same assistance from employment officials as nationals of the Member State. Having found employment EC nationals must report again to the authorities. For the issue of a residence permit they can be obliged to produce a passport or another document, a certificate of their employer and they may have to sign a statement with regard to their past record.

If the employment's certificate demonstrates that the duration of the **1.11** employment will be at least one year, a residence permit for five years should be issued. In case of employment for a period of three to twelve months, an EC national is entitled to a residence permit for the duration of the agreed employment. To EC nationals who will be working for more than three months the issue of a residence card is obligatory. For those working less, a simple stamp will suffice.

It is important to notice that the issue of an EC residence permit is a mere formality with a declaratory character; not the permit but the rules of Community law constitute the right to stay.

An EC residence card, which was issued for five years, should also be extended for five years. However, in cases of involuntary unemployment which has lasted for more than 12 months, the validity may be limited to one year at the first extension; if unemployment still prevails after this year, further extension can be refused.

Other possible circumstances which will put an end to someone's EC **1.12** residence status are: voluntary unemployment, a break of stay of more than six months or criminal behaviour. Military service, disability to work caused by illness or accident and involuntary unemployment will not affect EC residence status.

Termination of temporary employment as such is not a circumstance which will end EC status. In view of the European labour market it must be assumed that a worker is not in a position to freely choose between a temporary assignment and unlimited employment. The terms "worker" and "activity as an employed person" are determined by EC law and must be given a broad interpretation. According to the European Court of Justice the essential characteristics of employment are, that during a given time one person provides services for and under the direction of another in return for remuneration.

1.13   Part-time employment may very well constitute an EC residence status. The criterion is whether the job is "genuine and effective", irrespective of motives for taking employment or the level of income. Subsidiary means of subsistence supplied by public funds or private persons (family members) are irrelevant also, provided that the activities in employment are genuine and effective. The nature of the payment is not decisive either; room and board and a certain amount of pocket money can be considered as remuneration for activities in employment.

1.14   The nature of the job may determine whether the activities are genuine and effective; 15 hours per week of teaching may constitute genuine and effective employment, but a cleaning job for 10 hours a week may be disqualified as being marginal and secondary.

EC nationals have the right to be employed under the same statutory provisions which are applicable for the employment of national employees.

(ii) Business and self-employment

1.15   The right of establishment, laid down in Articles 52–59 of the EEC Treaty, confers the right of free movement on EC nationals wishing to enter a Member State in order to set up or manage a business or to become self-employed. This right extends to companies, legally incorporated in one of the Member States.

The implementation of the right of establishment has been carried out in Directive 73/148, giving similar rights to enter and to reside as those given to workers and their families in Directive 68/360. A whole set of Directives deals with the adequacy, standardisation and recognition of professional qualifications.

A five-year EC residence permit should be issued to a person who produces evidence that he/she established him/herself in business or in a self-employed occupation in the initial trial period of three to six months. Directive 75/34 gives business people and the self-employed the right to remain in the Member State after incapacity or retirement.

1.16   Two other Directives (90/364 and 90/365), confer as of 30 June 1992 the freedom of establishment on EC nationals who wish to take up residence in another Member State for purposes other than economic activities or for the purpose of retirement. Sufficient funds and health insurance are the main conditions. As such persons do not intend to be active in (self-)employment, these Directives embody a principal extension of the right of free movement. Non-active and retired EC nationals may be joined by household and dependent family members.

(iii) **Provision/reception of services**

Articles 59–66 give a right of free movement to EC nationals wishing to   **1.17**
provide services. The implementation can be found in Council Directive
73/148. Providers and recipients of services cannot claim lasting residence;
they have the right to leave their own country, enter the territory of another
Member State and remain there long enough to perform or receive the
intended services.

For visits of less than three months one would just need an identity card or
passport. For visits exceeding three months a residence card should be issued.

The right extends to persons who wish to travel in order to receive services.   **1.18**
The European Court of Justice held that the freedom to provide services
includes the freedom for the recipients of services to travel to another Member
State in order to receive a service there and that tourists, persons travelling for
business or educational purposes, and persons seeking medical treatment are
recipients of services.

In the *Rush Portuguesa* case the court has ruled, that a company, incorporated in a Member State, which provides services in another Member State,
may travel with its own staff which it brings from the main establishment for
the duration of the work. In such cases the authorities of the Member State on
whose territory the work is to be carried out may not impose conditions on the
provider of services as to the recruitment of workers on the spot or the
obtaining of a work permit for non-EC staff.

(iv) **EC students**

In the *Gravier* case the court has ruled that access to and participation in   **1.19**
courses of instruction and apprenticeship, in particular vocational training,
are connected to Community law. Any form of education which prepares for a
qualification for a particular profession, trade or employment or which
provides the necessary training and skills for such a profession, trade or
employment is vocational training, whatever the age and the level of training
of the pupils or students, and even if the training programme includes an
element of general education.

From this it follows that access to and participation in the general
educational system of a Member State does not fall within the scope of the EEC
Treaty. However, the children of EC workers or self-employed EC nationals
are to be admitted to the general education, apprenticeship and vocational
training courses of the host State under the same conditions as the nationals of
that State.

In 1990 the Council of Ministers laid down Directive 90/366 for EC   **1.20**
students. As from 1 July 1992 EC students are entitled to a residence permit
upon proof of matriculation at a university, college or educational institute for
the purpose of vocational training. Furthermore, they should have sufficient
funds to prevent them from becoming a public charge and have health
insurance for themselves, their eventual spouses and children, covering all risks
in the host State.

(v) **Members of the family**

1.21   The implementing provisions of EC law also confer the right of free movement upon:
- the spouse;
- children under 21;
- children over 21 who are still dependent on their parents;
- dependent grandchildren;
- non-dependent grandchildren of workers;
- dependent relatives in the ascending line, such as parents and grand-parents.

1.22   It must be assumed, that the term family members includes the descendants and ascendants of either spouse, and adopted children as well. The EC provisions stipulate that the Member States should facilitate the admission of other family members if they are dependent on the EC migrant or were living in the same household in their home country. Note, that these provisions for extended family reunion are reserved for EC nationals exercising the right of free movement; nationals of a Member State may be in a less favourable position.

1.23   Family members have the right to enter, to reside and to remain in the Member State where the EC migrant they are related to enjoys the right of free movement as a worker, self-employed person or as the provider or receiver of services. Non-EC family members are entitled to a residence document having the same validity as the document of the EC national with the primary right.

1.24   The person with the primary right should be able to offer housing which can be considered as regular according to the local standards and the legal family ties should remain intact. In the *Diatta* case the European Court of Justice ruled that the spouse of an EC national enjoying the right of free movement will keep the right to reside even if the household is no longer shared and divorce proceedings are pending.

Family members enjoy the same rights as the EC migrant they are related to, irrespective of nationality of sex. However, non-EC family members can be required to obtain an entry visa but the Member State has no discretion; the issue is a mere formality. Admitted family members have the right to take employment anywhere on the territory of the Member State, even at a place far removed from the residence of the EC migrant.

1.25   In the *Reed* case the European Court of Justice ruled that, if a Member State has made provisions for its own nationals to be joined by their unmarried "live in" partners, as is the case in The Netherlands, this social benefit cannot be denied to EC migrants.

A spouse will not lose the right to stay if on account of public policy, further stay is denied to the EC migrant to whom he/she is married. Although the EC status of the spouse has been derived from the person with the primary right, it is not to be regarded as a dependent status.

2. Limits on the right of free movement

Limits on the right of free movement may be imposed on the grounds of public **1.26** policy, public security or public health (Art 48 para 3, EEC Treaty).

In the Member States this public policy clause has been implemented in that a residence permit may be refused if an EC migrant is considered a risk to public peace, public security or public health. Refusal to renew or withdraw is possible in case of false information or infringements of public peace or public security.

Measures taken on the grounds of public policy or public security should be **1.27** based exclusively on the personal conduct of the individual concerned. A criminal conviction can be taken into account only in so far as the circumstances which gave rise to the conviction are evidence of personal conduct constituting a present threat to the requirements of public policy.

Diseases which may cause refusal of entry are listed in an annex to Directive 64/221. It may be worth mentioning that AIDS as such seems not to be included.

2. Limits on the right of free movement

Limits on the right of free movement may be imposed up to a certain acceptable... where public schools, of public schools, [who] [8] page... of 1990... T... [?] that, [?] [?] Since... the rule [?] ... [?] ... that a role allowing that it may be called school if pupils... a... [?] ... [?] large or public security or public health. Never may a... [?] ... be possible in case of flight... the intervention of the administrative power... may not be excessive...

Attention may be the amount of public... for under the service of public... [?] base on analysis on the present context of the rights guaranteed... [?] ... demand, cultivation was 10... [who] are... [?] ... [?] ... organizations to fight and to do the question to... [?] ... persons per year... Section 10 is particularly... presentation in the financial authority... to the rights. Due to section seems not related plenty of party an band... [?] ... by 30, to regard so with an changing. Sec. ArtDB p... that... [?] and nine...

Belgium

Chapter 2
Belgium

1. Permanent and temporary immigrants

The three instruments of Belgian law concerning labour and registration of **2.1**
foreign workers are the work permit, the profession card and the permission to
reside. They are described in this chapter together with the procedure for
obtaining each of them.

[*The next paragraph is 2.5.*]

(i) The work permit

The work permit governs the employment of persons bound by a contract of **2.5**
hire of labour or of persons who, otherwise than under the terms of such a
contract, work under the authority of another person.

In 1980 Belgium adopted a state structure similar to that of a federal state.
There are three regions: the Flemish region, the Walloon region and the region
of Brussels-Capital. The issue of work permits has been entrusted to the
Executives of these regions, depending on whether the worker will carry out his
activities in Flanders, in the Walloon provinces or in Brussels.

Presently the regulation of work permits is uniform throughout Belgium. In **2.6**
the future, however, it could be modified region by region.

On 1 August 1974, the Cabinet decided to stop, temporarily, new **2.7**
immigration of workers from non-EC Member Countries. This decision is still
applicable. There are, however, certain exceptions, notably in favour of highly
qualified persons.

The basic principles

According to the Royal Decree No. 34 of 20 July 1967 concerning the **2.8**
employment of workers of foreign nationality, no employer may employ a
worker who does not have Belgian nationality, without having obtained an
employment licence beforehand from the Ministry of the Flemish, Walloon or
Brussels-Capital region, according to the place of employment.

Similarly, no worker of a foreign nationality may work without being
covered by a work permit.

The "worker" is defined as: the person bound by a contract of hire of labour **2.9**
or who, otherwise than under the terms of such a contract, works under the
authority of another person. As a consequence, trainees must hold a work
permit and their employer should possess an employment licence.

This decree is, however, not applicable for:
- journalists residing in Belgium and exclusively attached to newspapers published abroad;
- commercial travellers who have their main residence abroad and who visit their clients in Belgium on account of firms established abroad, which do not have branches in Belgium, as long as their stay in Belgium does not exceed three months in succession;
- persons who enter Belgium in order to receive merchandise delivered by a Belgian business, on account of a business established abroad, as long as their stay in the country does not exceed three months in succession.

These workers need not hold a work permit. The "employer" is defined as: the person who employs the workers.

The different categories of work permits

2.10 There are three types of work permit:
- (i) work permit A, valid for all employers and for all professions for an indefinite period;
- (ii) work permit B, valid for a specific employer and for a maximum period of one year;
- (iii) work permit C, valid for certain specific jobs for which the person could have several employers (home workers, jockeys, charwomen).

Conditions for granting work permits

WORK PERMIT A

2.11 Three criteria are taken into consideration:
2.12 (i) the criterion of residence:
- the worker who gives proof of five years' regular and uninterrupted residence in Belgium;
- political refugees acknowledged in Belgium who can give proof of three years' regular and uninterrupted residence in Belgium;

2.13 (ii) the work criterion:
- the nationals of countries[1], with which Belgium is bound by a work agreement, who give proof of three years' work covered by a work permit during a regular and uninterrupted stay. This proof must be given during the period which immediately precedes the date of the request;
- political refugees who can give proof of three working years covered by a work permit and a regular permission to reside;
- nationals of other countries who can give proof of four years' work;

2.14 (iii) the family criterion:
- for the husband/wife living under the same roof as the worker who has the right to obtain work permit A;

––––––

[1] Algeria, Austria, Spain, Iceland, Malta, Poland, Morocco, Norway, Portugal and Turkey.

- for the husband/wife, who is an EC national, living under the same roof as a worker who is also an EC national;
- for legal or adoptive children, who are single and aged under 21, of the worker who has the right to obtain work permit A, on condition that the husband/wife also lives in Belgium under the same roof as the worker and that the children arrived in Belgium at the same time as the parents or at the latest six months after the arrival of the last partner in Belgium;
- for the natural, adoptive or legal children, who are single and aged under 21, of the worker who has the right to obtain work permit A and who live under the same roof, if the worker is single, a widower or divorced and if the children arrived in Belgium at the same time as the worker or at the latest six months after the arrival of the latter in Belgium;
- for the husband/wife and children of the worker, if the latter stayed regularly in Belgium and had the right to obtain a work permit A at the moment of his/her death;
- for some exceptional cases, the competent minister can raise the age limit of 21 years to 25 years.

WORK PERMIT B

The work permit will be granted: **2.15**
- if the employment licence and the work permit relate to a national of a country with which Belgium is bound by a convention or an international agreement of manual labour;
- if the work permit and the employment licence concern a worker able to do a job in a satisfactory way and within a reasonable term, and a post that cannot be filled by workers from the national labour market.

The granting of an employment licence and a work permit related to a **2.16** worker who does not regularly reside in Belgium, is subordinate to the signature by the two parties of a standard contract (see below the procedure for the granting of work permits A and B).

The procedure for the granting of work permits A and B
IF THE WORKER RESIDES ABROAD OR DOES NOT REGULARLY STAY IN BELGIUM AND THIS IS THE FIRST TIME HE/SHE HAS WORKED IN BELGIUM

The Royal Decree No. 34 of the 20 July 1967 states that a worker who does not **2.17** have Belgian nationality cannot enter Belgium, in order to work in the country, without having first obtained a work permit. It is, therefore, the potential employer who should submit the request for a work permit to the competent labour administration in Belgium. The work permit is correctly entitled an "employment licence".

The following medical documents must be attached to the request: **2.18**
- a medical certificate attesting, on the basis of a general examination, that

15

the worker does not have a contagious or transmittable disease and that nothing indicates that his/her state of health will make him/her unfit for work in the near future;

— a serological examination;

— an X-ray examination of the lungs.

2.19 The medical certificate must be drawn up by a doctor approved by the diplomatic and consular authorities of the country where the worker resides.

The request must also contain a copy of the standard labour contract, the text of which was drawn up in the Royal Decree of 5 May 1970. The employer must collect this contract from the competent Regional Employment Exchange. The contract must be signed by both parties.

IF THE WORKER HAS STAYED REGULARLY IN BELGIUM OVER A PERIOD OF LESS THAN TWO YEARS AND THIS IS THE FIRST TIME HE/SHE HAS WORKED IN BELGIUM (*i.e.* he/she does not yet hold a work permit)

2.20 The request must be accompanied by:

— a medical certificate;

— an information sheet.

The last document should contain information concerning the length of the sojourn of the worker in Belgium and also the composition of his family.

2.21 This data is necessary for fixing the period of validity of the work permit. Again, the request must be made by the employer.

IF THE WORKER HAS RESIDED REGULARLY IN BELGIUM FOR MORE THAN TWO YEARS, AND IF HE/SHE IS NOW WORKING FOR THE FIRST TIME IN BELGIUM AS A WAGE EARNER

2.22 The request need only be accompanied by an information sheet (see above) which, again, should be submitted by the employer.

IF THE WORKER REGULARLY RESIDES IN BELGIUM AND IF HE/SHE IS ALREADY THE HOLDER: of a work permit B, valid for a specific employer or a work permit B for a specific field of activity, different from the sector in which the worker is now to be employed.

2.23 In this case, the employer must submit a new request for a work permit, accompanied by an information sheet.

Renewal of the work permit

2.24 The work permit A is granted for an indeterminate period. The work permit, however, becomes invalid if the worker leaves the Kingdom for a period of more than one year.

The only work permits which are subject to renewal are, therefore, work permits B and C, for which the duration is limited.

Work permit B is valid for a period from one to five years, according to the   **2.25**
field of activity. The renewal of the permit can be granted as long as the worker
stays in the field of activity for which he obtained his first work permit.

Work permit C is granted for a period that is dependent upon the duration
of the employment of the worker. The conditions for the renewal are identical
to those of work permit B.

Appeals

If a request for a work permit is refused, an appeal can be addressed to the   **2.26**
competent minister, and later to the Council of State.

(ii) The profession card

The profession card governs the practice of a profitable and independent   **2.27**
activity on Belgian territory. It is granted under the authority of the Belgian
Government, the Minister of the Middle Classes being the official responsible.

The basic principle

The practice of a profitable and independent activity is dependent upon the   **2.28**
grant of a profession card.

Certain categories of workers are, however, exempt:
(i)   the wife of the worker whose professional activity is limited by the
       support she gives to her husband in the exercise of his profession;
(ii)   the professional sportsman whose activities do not exceed more than 60
       days per year;
(iii) musicians and artists who perform in a theatre, a circus or a hall
       exclusively for shows, as long as the duration of the sojourn in Belgium
       for their performance does not exceed 15 days per half-year; and
(iv)   foreigners residing abroad, who make business trips to Belgium which
       cumulatively do not exceed three months per half-year.

"Business trips" are defined as journeys made in Belgium by foreigners who   **2.29**
do not reside in Belgium and who intend to visit tradesmen, industrial or
commercial agents who are their correspondents; or who offer their services for
research and study; or who propose to establish relations in order to encourage
international trade, on condition that they have not set up a depot in the
country or at the customs.

The following are also considered as business trips: **2.30**
(a)   participation in commercial fairs and exhibitions, as long as the products
       exhibited are samples which will not be sold by the exhibitor to private
       persons for their private use;
(b)   journeys made in Belgium by foreigners who do not effectively take part
       in the daily administration of a firm, but who visit in order to participate
       in a meeting of a board of directors or in a general meeting of a trading
       company.

17

Conditions for granting the profession card

2.31   (i)   The granting of the profession card is linked to the worker's permission to reside.

       (ii)   The activity must not be carried out in a field of economic activity that has already reached saturation point. The Minister of the Middle Classes has full powers of judgment to rule on this matter.

      (iii)   The foreigner who has been refused a profession card is only authorised to submit a new request for the same activity after a period of two years from the date of submission of his previous request, unless a new fact appears.

Procedure for granting the profession card

IF THE WORKER DOES NOT RESIDE IN BELGIUM

2.32   The request for a profession card must be submitted to the Belgian diplomatic and consular authorities in the country in which the worker last resided, at the same time as the request for a visa for temporary residence or permission to reside.

Foreigners who reside in Belgium with permission to reside other than the identity card for foreigners, the certificate of registration in the foreigners' register or the certificate of registration model A, file their appeal to the Belgian diplomatic and consular service of the country of their last residence.

IF THE WORKER RESIDES IN BELGIUM

2.33   Foreigners authorised to reside in Belgium, holders of a foreign identity card, a certificate of registration in the foreigners' register, or a certificate of registration model A, and also refugees recognised by the United Nations, must introduce their requests for the acquisition of a profession card at the municipal administration of the place of their residence.

FORMALITIES FOR SUBMITTING A REQUEST FOR A PROFESSION CARD

2.34   The request may only be drawn up on the forms obtainable from the Belgian diplomatic or consular services and the municipal administrations.

The person making the application is obliged to sign personally his request for a profession card.

On the request, he has to indicate:
- the exact nature of the activity;
- the place where the activity will be carried out.

2.35   He will also have to produce the following documents:
- a certificate of good character;
- a medical certificate drawn up by a doctor appointed by an authorised Belgian diplomatic or consular agent.

THE EXAMINATION OF THE REQUEST FOR THE ACQUISITION OF A PROFESSION CARD

There are two different procedures for the examination of the acquisition of a profession card: **2.36**

(i)   A direct and quick procedure at the end of which the card can be granted straight away. This will happen either if the required opinions are all favourable, if the interested person has resided for more than five years in Belgium, or if the activity is not carried out in an area subject to restrictions, or if the economic activity belongs to the categories privileged by the economic interest they represent as far as investments or labour are concerned, or by the fact that the activity is limited in time and highly qualified, or that the foreigner belongs to one of the following categories: **2.37**

   (a)   the worker has married a person who has Belgian nationality; or

   (b)   the worker fell victim in Belgium to an industrial accident which prevented him/her from carrying on his/her salaried activity; or

   (c)   the worker fulfils the legal conditions for the acquisition, by option, of Belgian nationality and has introduced an official request for this purpose; or

   (d)   the worker is a political refugee.

(ii)   A procedure that requires the opinion of the Board for economic enquiry of foreigners which gives audience to the explanations of the foreigner. The latter can be accompanied or represented by a lawyer. **2.38**

This procedure is required when the administration considers that there are sufficient reasons for the refusal of the profession card, in particular, when it concerns a new immigrant, or if the activity belongs to a saturated field of activity, even when the applicant has not resided in Belgium for more than five years, or when the file contains several negative advices founded either on the personal situation of the worker, or on economic data.

At the end of this opinion procedure, the decision concerning the request for a profession card is principally made in accordance with the opinion of the Board of enquiry. If the administration deviates from this opinion, it will hand over the file to the competent minister for a decision.

The opinions asked for during the examination of the request, come, on the one hand, from the Foreigners' Office of the Department of Justice, and, on the other, from the municipal administration affected by the application, or the trade administration of the Ministry of Foreign Affairs if it concerns an activity related to import-export or the wholesale and industrial sector.

THE GRANTING OF THE PROFESSION CARD

The profession card granted to a foreigner is handed over to the municipal or diplomatic or consular Belgian authority, according to the place where the request was made. **2.39**

Its handing over is subject to the receipt of payment/fee (1,000 F at the present time). If the card is valid for more than one year, the amount is multiplied by a number equal to the total amount of years, plus a fraction for any supplementary years for which the card is granted.

The renewal of the profession card

2.40 The maximum period for which a profession card is valid is five years. At the end of this period, the card can be renewed.

At the time of submission of a renewal form, the foreigner must attach various certificates proving that he has fulfilled his fiscal duties and that he has paid the contributions he owes to the Social Security Service for self-employed persons.

(iii) Permission to reside

2.41 The sojourn of foreigners on Belgian territory is governed by the Law of 15 December 1980 on the access to territory, residence, settlement and removal of foreigners.

This law distinguishes three categories of permission to reside:
– the short sojourn which does not exceed three months;
– the sojourn; and
– the establishment.

2.42 The carrying out of a salaried or self-employed activity by a foreigner is linked to the permission to reside.

This right is nevertheless granted under the terms of a separate procedure from the work permit and the profession card. Consequently the foreigner must hold these two licences.

The short sojourn

2.43 Access to the territory is subject to the production of a visa. However, this is not required for EC nationals and nationals of countries with which Belgium has entered into an agreement of reciprocity.

The sojourn

2.44 The worker who is an EC national must always obtain authorisation to stay on the Kingdom's territory, before coming to Belgium. This authorisation is left to the discretion of the Home Secretary who does not have to justify his refusal with particular grounds.

2.45 Certain foreigners are, however, allowed to stay *ipso jure*.
(i)   The foreigner for whom the right to sojourn is recognised by an international treaty, by the law or by a royal decree.
(ii) The foreigner who fulfils the legal conditions, other than those related to residence, in order to acquire Belgian nationality or to recover this nationality.
(iii) The woman, Belgian by birth, who, by her marriage or as a result of the acquisition of a husband of foreign nationality, has lost Belgian nationality.

(iv)   The foreign spouse of a foreigner admitted or authorised to sojourn in the Kingdom or authorised to establish him/herself there, who is coming to live with him/her, as well as their children if they are dependent on them and if they came to live with them before their eighteenth birthday, unless an international treaty binding Belgium offers more favourable conditions. The right to invoke family regrouping has been limited in order to avoid a gradual regrouping.

With the exception of the cases detailed above, non-EC nationals may thus not reside on Belgium territory unless they obtain a permission to reside which is granted to them on the basis of article 9 of the Law of 15 December 1980.

Some foreigners still benefit from access facilities to the territory or from the right to sojourn:

STUDENTS

Students can be authorised to sojourn for the term of their studies on the **2.46** territory of the Kingdom, as long as they enter upon or continue higher education or a preparatory year for higher education.

Higher education is defined as studies after the General Certificate of Education.

Among the documents that have to be produced in support of the request to sojourn, there must be a document that proves that the student has sufficient means of subsistence.

Members of the family of the student are authorised to join him/her on condition that he/she proves that he/she has sufficient means of subsistence to welcome them and that he/she has the necessary accommodation.

BUSINESSMEN

Businessmen who do not desire to sojourn in Belgium for more than three **2.47** months, can obtain for short trips to Belgium, a business visa valid for one year.

This document allows access to the territory for one year as long as the cumulated different sojourns do not exceed 180 days.

AU PAIRS

No special regime has been developed for this category of persons. They may **2.48** not, therefore, sojourn unless they have been explicitly authorised to do so.

The establishment

The right to establish has been granted to persons authorised to sojourn on the **2.49** territory of the Kingdom and who have resided there for two years.

The request has to be made at the municipal administration of the place of residence.

The procedure for permission to reside

The request for a permission to reside must be obtained at the Belgian **2.50** diplomatic service of the place of the last residence of the worker, except for workers allowed to stay *ipso jure*.

Once in possession of a temporary permission to reside and of the work permit or profession card, the foreigner is authorised to stay in Belgium for (in principle) an unlimited period.

2.51 When he/she arrives in Belgium he/she must be registered with the municipality of the place of his/her residence.

Afterwards, the worker can ask for establishment.

A certificate states that the permission to reside of the worker must be renewed at the end of its validity, which can be one to five years. The validity of this certificate is independent of the permission to reside, a permission which is granted for an unlimited period.

2. Asylum

2.52 Asylum is granted to the foreigner who meets the criteria enumerated in paragraph 1 of the international treaty relating to refugee status, signed at Geneva on 28 July 1951. Asylum is also granted to persons who benefit from refugee status, if this status has been obtained prior to the Geneva treaty. The refugee who obtained refugee status in a foreign country can keep this status if it is confirmed by the competent Belgian authorities.

2.53 In order to contain the stream of refugees, the procedure for granting refugee status has been split into two stages. During the first stage, the request is examined roughly. In cases of refusal, the refugee can be expelled from the territory. Several procedures allow the candidate to enforce his rights. The second stage, which is reserved to candidates that have not been expelled, concerns the complete consideration of the demand by an organisation which is independent of the Belgian Authorities. Appeals are permitted in cases of refusal of refugee status.

3. Nationality

2.54 Belgian nationality can be obtained by:
- attribution, owing to a Belgian relative;
- birth in Belgium;
- option, in particular because of marriage;
- naturalisation, after a certain number of years of residence.

4. Sanctions

2.55 Illegal sojourn in Belgium can lead at one and the same time to a penalty and a deportation order. In order to ensure the efficiency of this last measure, the foreigner can be placed at the disposal of the government and imprisoned.

2.56 Among the deportation measures are an order to leave the territory, or repatriation or actual expulsion. Once an order to leave the territory has been served this does not prevent a return to the territory of the Kingdom, after the situation of the sojourn has been regularised. However, repatriation or expulsion prohibits a return during a certain period, determined by the repatriation or expulsion order.

EC nationals can only be expelled or repatriated if they seriously violate law and order.

Denmark

Chapter 3
Denmark

Introduction

(i) Immigration policy

Danish immigration policy is very much influenced by the fact that the **3.1** country borders the Nordic countries on the one side, and Germany/the EC countries on the other. The Danish Aliens Act divides foreign nationals into three main categories; nationals from the other Nordic countries, nationals from countries belonging to the European Community, and nationals from from the so-called "third countries".

(a) Nationals from other Nordic countries

According to section 1 of the Danish Aliens Act, citizens from Finland, **3.2** Iceland, Norway and Sweden can enter and reside temporarily or permanently in Denmark without seeking permission. It is because of this agreement between these countries that Nordic citizens do not even have to be in possession of a passport while travelling between these countries. Furthermore, nationals from other Nordic countries do not need a work permit if they want to take up paid or unpaid work in Denmark.

(b) All other nationals

In contrast to the liberal rules of entry and residence applying to nationals **3.3** from Nordic countries, *all* other foreign nationals who intend to reside permanently must apply for a residence permit. Since 1969 restrictions on granting such permission have been in force. As a result of a sudden rise in unemployment due to the oil crisis in 1972–73, a general ban on immigration was introduced, and has been in force ever since.

(c) EC nationals

A major exception to this ban is nationals coming from Member States of the **3.4** European Community. Denmark joined the Community almost at the same time as the ban on immigration was introduced, and consequently nationals of the other Community countries have a legal right to obtain employment in Denmark without restrictions (like requirements of a work permit etc). If the EC national, however, fails to find a job, he or she is obliged to leave the country after a period of three months. Community visitors and tourists, who do not perform any professional activities, can also enter and stay for three months without any restrictions.

From this it appears that citizens from other Community Member States have the same opportunities of temporary residence in Denmark as nationals from Nordic countries. However, the possibility of residence for more than three months is restricted in general to those performing professional activities. The rules applying to EC nationals are more specifically described at paras 3.45–3.50.

3.5   While Community nationals have a legal right to seek employment in Denmark, the overall intention of the immigration ban is to prevent nationals from the so-called "third countries" taking up work in Denmark.

In this chapter the *very* limited exceptions to the general ban on immigration are described.

(ii) Foreign nationals from outside the European Community and Nordic countries

3.6   The Danish Aliens Act distinguishes between foreign nationals who intend to enter Denmark temporarily and those who intend to reside permanently. Furthermore, the rules divide foreigners into two groups dependent on their nationalities: those included in the annual visa list, and those not included.

All foreign nationals must make up their minds, before arrival, whether they intend to stay temporarily or permanently in Denmark.

(a) Permanent residence

3.7   If foreign nationals want permanent residence they must apply in advance according to the few limited possibilities in the Aliens Act, like, for example, family reunification (listed at paras 3.20–3.28).

(b) Temporary visits

3.8   Those nationals who do not need a visa, and who intend to stay temporarily, can enter the country if they hold a valid passport. The frontier control, however, can deny entry if there is reason to believe that the foreign person intends to reside permanently or take up work, for example if that specific person is not in possession of a minimum amount of money to pay the costs of a temporary visit.

Those nationals who need a visa before entry can apply for reasons such as business meetings, participation in cultural or scientific arrangements or tourism (in relation to temporary work or education see paras 3.11–3.18).

3.9   The granting of a visa can be rejected if the Danish authorities have reason to believe that the stay is going to be permanent. Even though a visa is granted, the border control is authorised to reject the foreign person if there is reason to believe that the visit is not going to be temporary.

There has been a general trend in Danish visa policy, to lay down visa requirements for countries from which a number of visitors have "changed their minds" and after arrival have asked for political asylum, or have married etc.

In the following sections the rules concerning residence and the work permit **3.10** are described simultaneously because of the very close connection between these two kinds of permits.

1. Permanent immigrants

(i) Employment

(a) "The Rule of specialists"

The main reason for this provision is to maintain the possibility of allowing the **3.11** assistance of foreign workers, in the interest of the Danish society.

In relation to the ordinary labour market this provision is only used to solve **3.12** major problems concerning employment or problems of a commercial character. It is a precondition, that the foreign person is qualified to do this particular kind of job which no one in Denmark is qualified to do, and that it is urgent according to the interests of production. In such cases a work permit and consequently residence permit are granted. This residence permit, however, is usually granted for the purpose of a temporary stay. Furthermore, the residence permit is given on the condition that the person only works at a specified task or for a particular employer. If these conditions change, for instance, if the person is offered another job, a new application form must be filled in and approved by the authorities before the person can take up the new job.

Outside the ordinary labour market, special rules apply to a number of working-categories such as the following.

(b) Businessmen/women

Residence permits in connection with the establishment of a private firm, are **3.13** only granted if the establishment of the firm serves special Danish interests. Such interests are *not* constituted by the mere fact that investment is made or more jobs are created in Denmark. Permits are very seldom granted to retailers or owners of restaurants etc.

(c) Trainees

Trainees between the ages of 18 and 30 can be granted a residence permit for **3.14** 18 months. The permit may be extended to cover a period of two years. Denmark has made special stay-agreements with certain countries concerning exchange of trainees. Permission to work is not granted unless the work is an integrated part of the programme.

(d) Senior employees of foreign firms

Permits are granted for directors, heads of technical or administrative **3.15** departments of local branches in Denmark.

(e) Housemaids in private households

3.16 Residence permits are granted for a maximum period of two years, and cannot be extended. Permission is only granted if that specific household usually employs housemaids and it provides food and accommodation and pays a minimum salary according to Danish standards.

(f) Instructors, erectors etc

3.17 Danish firms buying technical equipment which needs installation or instruction can invite foreign instructors, erectors etc for a three-month period. At the end of this period it is necessary to apply for work and residence permits. If a visa is required on arrival, the Danish authorities consider this visa application in relation to information received from the Danish firm.

(g) Education

3.18 Professors, teachers and scientific employees can be employed for a three-month period without work permits. Persons coming from countries from which visas are required must apply in advance. Residence permits are not demanded in cases of temporary stays with a maximum of three months. This applies whether the person comes from a country from which visas are required or not.

In the case of residence for more than three months, residence permits are required for all third country nationals.

(ii) Persons who used to have Danish citizenship

3.19 Pursuant to section 9.1.1 of the Aliens Act foreign nationals, who have had Danish citizenship before, have a legal claim for a residence permit. The major category consists of Danish citizens who by marriage changed citizenship and left the country.

For all persons coming from third countries, except refugees, a work permit is required to take up work. This also includes former Danish citizens. After five years of permanent residence in Denmark, however, a work permit is no longer required.

(iii) Family reunification (nuclear family)

(a) Foreign nationals

3.20 Foreign nationals who have been living legally in Denmark for five years have a legal right to apply for family reunification with *spouses*. It is up to the couple to provide a marriage certificate or similar documentation from the country of origin to prove that the marriage is lawful. At the same time, however, the marriage must not conflict with basic Danish standards (a husband lawfully married to two wives according to the traditions of the country of origin, is not allowed to be reunified with both wives). The question of family reunification causes a good deal of political disturbance in Denmark. Opponents to the rule claim that many naturalised foreigners in Denmark use the rule to introduce spouses hitherto unknown to them from their former home countries in spite of the restrictions on immigration.

(b) Common law marriage

Persons who have been living together in a stable marriage-like relationship **3.21** (common law marriage) for at least one and a half to two years, have the right of reunification under the same conditions as mentioned before. Such common law marriages are usually heterosexual, but homosexual partnerships are also accepted by Danish law.

In both situations it is required that the person residing in Denmark is able to provide for the family, according to Danish standards, and that both persons have reached the age of 18.

(c) Formal engagements

It must be noted that formal engagements do *not* qualify for family **3.22** reunification (unless there has been such a prior common law marriage as mentioned above). Furthermore, it is almost impossible to be granted a visitors' visa if the Danish authorities receive information that the applicant intends to marry a person who has permanent residence in Denmark. In one case, however, the Danish Ombudsman criticised this practice, because the person residing in Denmark was a refugee and consequently he was prevented from returning to his country of origin to be married to his fiancée there.

In contrast, permanent immigrants who reside permanently in Denmark **3.23** and have this possibility , must return to their country of origin to be married, and then apply for family reunification with him or her.

(d) Children under 18

Furthermore, there is a right of reunification with one's *underage children*. The **3.24** definition of "underage" follows the Danish standard which means children under the age of 18 years. The applicants must provide the Danish authorities with documentation like, for example, a birth certificate to prove that the child is underage. Reasonable flexibility is rendered in relation to legislation and administration in the country of origin which might make it impossible to produce such documentation.

(e) Parents

With regard to reunification with the parents of a person who has resided in **3.25** Denmark for more than five years, this can be allowed when the parents reach the age of 65. It is required that the residing person is able to support the parents when they arrive in Denmark. If the parents have other children in their country of origin, permission for reunification is not granted.

Those persons who are granted a permanent residence permit in accordance with the rules of family reunification can apply for a work permit. Spouses or children are usually granted such permission, whilst normally parents are denied a work permit.

(g) Foreigners

3.26 Pursuant to section 9.2 of the Aliens Act foreigners who apply in the following situations can be granted a residence permit, but it is not a legal right. When a person fulfills the requirements in the following situations, it is said that the Danish authorities have an optional power of granting residence permits.

OTHER FAMILY-LIKE RELATIONS

3.27 Foreign nationals having family relations other than the relationships mentioned in section 9.1 (nuclear family) or similar close connections to a person living permanently in Denmark, can obtain residence permits. The intention of this provision is to create the possibility of reunification between a permanent resident and a person that the resident is under an obligation to support because of a prior foster-parent relationship etc.

ADOPTION OF FOREIGN CHILDREN

3.28 In connection with adoption of foreign children by Danish citizens, the children are granted Danish citizenship automatically if the child – as in the majority of cases – is under 12 years of age. Children above that age will become Danish citizens provided they express their interest in becoming so.

(iv) Family reunification (non-nuclear) other relatives

3.29 It must be stressed, that the provision does not open up possibilities of reunification with (nuclear) family members who fall outside the scope of section 9.1, like children over the age of 18 years, parents under the age of 65, sisters or brothers, uncles etc.

Those family members have no possibilities of reunification at all. Furthermore, close family members from visa restricted countries often have difficulties in obtaining a visitors visa because the authorities fear that they intend to reside permanently with their relatives.

2. Special circumstances

3.30 While the prior provision concerned exceptions from the ban on emigration to meet Danish demands, the last provision in section 9 of the Aliens Act opens the possibility of taking into account the special circumstances of the applicant.

(i) Students

3.31 Students coming from Third World countries on special educational programmes sponsored by the Danish Ministry of Foreign Affairs are guaranteed residence. Residence permits are also granted in order to receive an education only provided by Danish educational establishments. Finally, the provision opens up provision for an exchange of students arranged by Danish and foreign organisations. If a foreign student wants to receive further or higher education after having completed the education on the basis of which he or she was granted the residence permit, a renewal of the permit is not automatically given. If there is a natural link between the two education courses a new permit may be granted.

The main rule concerning work is that the students are denied work permits. **3.32** As an exception, however, students are allowed to work in the months of June, July and August. After 18 months they can be granted permission to work for a maximum of 15 hours a week.

(ii) **Temporary workers**

(a) Au pairs

Au pairs can be granted residence permits for a maximum period of two years. **3.33** In general, permission is only granted to nationals from Nordic and EC countries or countries of a similar standard of development. Under special circumstances permits might also be granted to persons coming from Third World countries.

(b) Ministers of religion

Ministers connected with non-state religious communities operating in **3.34** Denmark can be granted temporary residence permits for a maximum of two years.

(iii) **Further special circumstances**

Finally it should be pointed out that residence permits may be granted on the **3.35** basis of a provision if special circumstances are present, for example a previous long-term residence in Denmark or a long employment period with a Danish firm abroad. The application of this provision is extremely restricted.

In this connection, it must be noted, that even though the immigration ban was introduced due to rising unemployment, Danish policy does not allow foreign persons to enter Denmark with the purpose of staying during their retirement. It makes no difference that they are not performing any professional activities and are able to pay all the costs related to their residence in Denmark. The only exception to this is cases of family reunification.

3. **Refugees and political asylum**

Asylum seekers entering Denmark have a right to stay in Denmark, if they fall **3.36** within the provisions of the UN Convention Relating to the Status of Refugees of 1951. Applicants, however, are also granted asylum when reasons similar to those listed in the convention are in question or there are other weighty reasons why the alien should not be required to return to his/her home country. If (typically) a man is granted asylum by the Directorate for Aliens, his accompanying wife and children are automatically granted a permanent residence permit too. If the family is still in the country of origin, they have the right of family reunification. In case of refusal, the applicant has a right of appeal to the Refugee Appeals Board. The Board can change the decision and grant asylum or it can agree with the decision of the Directorate.

3.37　　In a very limited number of cases the Ministry of Justice can permit residence due to "special humanitarian reasons". So far these permits have primarily been given to families with underage children coming from war-ridden areas. If the applicant is refused by the Appeal Board and the Ministry of Justice, then he and any accompanying family members are obliged to leave the country; if not voluntarily then with the assistance of the police.

　　There is no possibility, like the German "Duldung", that the applicant can stay after the final refusal by the Appeal Board.

Asylum seekers

3.38　　Asylum seekers waiting for the authorities' final decision are not allowed to take up paid or unpaid work. If asylum is granted the refugee does not need a work permit, and can seek employment on equal terms with Danes.

4. Nationality

3.39　　To obtain Danish citizenship, it is necessary that the applicant has been residing in Denmark for at least seven years and at present resides in the country. Furthermore, a good knowledge of the Danish language is required, and the persons involved must be ready to give up their former citizenship.

　　Criminal offences and receipt of social benefits that are to be repaid to the Danish state, normally postpone the granting of citizenship.

3.40　　More liberal rules granting Danish citizenship apply to foreigners who have been married to Danish citizens for at least three years. If this is the case, only four years of permanent residence is required before an application can be filed.

　　With regard to refugees, six years of permanent residence from the date they were granted refugee status is required before an application can be filed.

　　Citizens of Finland, Norway and Sweden who have resided permanently in Denmark for seven years have a legal claim to citizenship. In general, other foreign persons cannot acquire Danish citizenship, unless through marriage to a Danish citizen. Furthermore, persons who have lived permanently in Denmark for five years prior to reaching the age of 16, can acquire Danish citizenship by handing in a special application form. This must be done before reaching the age of 23.

5. **Sanctions**

(i) **Denial of entry at the border or expulsion**

Foreigners who do not fulfill the legal requirements on arrival, like holding **3.41**
valid passports or visas when required, are denied entry at the border. If such a
person claims to be an asylum applicant, the police are not authorised to deny
entry in the first place. In such situations the decision of denial is taken by the
Directorate for Aliens. They assess whether the applicant will be expelled to a
country where there is a risk of persecution. If there is no such fear, the person is
denied entry by the Directorate. This decision, however, can be appealed to
the Minister of Justice. Such an appeal does not have suspensive effect.

Foreigners holding a valid passport, visa etc are usually allowed entry **3.42**
without further requirements. The Danish border control, however, is
authorised to ask whether the holders of, for example a tourist visa are in
possession of an adequate amount of money to cover all expenses in the period
for which the visa is valid. The authorities may deny them entry at the border
otherwise.

(ii) **Withdrawal of residence permit**

If a foreign person has been permitted entry to the country with the intention **3.43**
of permanent residence, Danish law provides a far reaching protection against
having the residence permit withdrawn. If the reasons for giving the permit
have ceased to exist, the general rule in the Aliens Act is that the permission
can be withdrawn. If a person, however, has stayed legally in the country for
three years, with the intention of permanent residence, the residence permit
cannot be withdrawn, even if the reasons for giving it have ceased. The most
common example is when a couple gets a divorce more than three years after
the time when family reunification was permitted. If the information given by
the applicant was false, the permission can always be withdrawn.

(iii) **Expulsion**

In criminal cases a decision to expel a foreign national from the country can be **3.44**
part of the court verdict. In the Aliens Act a special direction of the reasons
why foreign citizens can be expelled is given. The principle followed is that the
longer a foreign national has stayed in Denmark, the more serious the crime
that must be committed in order to be expelled.

France

Chapter 4
France

Introduction

Although immigration regulations have become considerably more stringent **4.1**
since 1975, France continues to remain quite open to visitors and residents
with valuable skills, independent means, or close family relations in France.

As a signatory member of the Treaty of Rome, France makes an important
distinction between nationals of the European Community and other
nationals, with regards to the immigration of persons offering or receiving
services, such as workers and students. Immigration procedures have been
simplified for EC nationals benefiting from the favourable conditions of the
Treaty, but continue to be bureaucratically complex and time-consuming for
other EC nationals and most non-EC nationals.

The outward appearance of the applications and supporting documents is **4.2**
very important and immigration officers may use discretion in accepting
applications that do not fully comply with the requirements.

1. Permanent immigrants

All non-French nationals who intend to live in France for more than three **4.3**
months must obtain a residence permit (*carte de séjour*) at the designated town
hall, police station, or préfecture of the intended place of residence of the
applicant in France.

Before leaving their country of residence for France, most non-EC nationals
wishing to live in France must obtain a long-stay visa, which will be used to
apply for a residence card upon arrival in France and will determine their
future residence status and authorisation to work. Non-EC nationals entering
France as tourists are not eligible to work or stay for more than three months,
since they lack the obligatory long-stay visa. EC nationals may ordinarily
enter as tourists and apply for a work permit within the first three months of
their arrival.

Non-EC nationals are granted a renewable one-year residence permit,
while EC nationals receive a five-year EC residence permit (see paras
4.13–4.14).

Holders of temporary residence permits for three consecutive years are **4.4**
eligible for a 10-year work and residence permit (see paras 4.15–4.17).

Holders of residence permits that do not permit employment may apply in
France for authorisation to work only by changing their working status

39

through a lengthy bureaucratic process known as "regularisation", which can take up to six months, with no guarantee of success.

4.5   A medical examination in the country of residence by a consulate-approved doctor is usually obligatory for non-EC nationals, and authorisation to reside in France will be refused to persons diagnosed with illnesses that are deemed to endanger public health, security, or law and order.

(i) Employment

(a) Non-EC nationals

COMBINED WORK AND RESIDENCE PERMIT (*Carte Unique de Séjour et de Travail*)

4.6   In order to live and work as an employee in France for more than one year, non-EC nationals must obtain a residence permit (*carte de séjour*) and a work permit (*carte de travail*). These two permits are issued jointly in the form of a combined work and residence permit (*carte unique de séjour et de travail*).

The combined work and residence permit is valid for one year and is renewable yearly for a maximum of two additional years. This permit may be subject to geographical limitations, particularly for applicants in lower-echelon jobs.

4.7   Authorisation to work can be obtained relatively easily by senior executives with a salary of at least 13 times the legal minimum wage (including contractual fringe benefits, bonuses and other related employee benefits) or highly qualified employees with valuable technical expertise.

The employer must normally apply for a long-stay visa while the prospective employee is still abroad. An undetermined-term work contract is required and the employment must be bona fide. Although the work may be full- or part-time, the minimum contractual salary of regular employees should not be less than four times the legal minimum wage (currently, the salary must be 22,000 FF per month). The employee must demonstrate that he can obtain adequate housing in France.

4.8   In the case of refusal to grant a work permit, administrative authorities are required to give the applicant a written statement of the reasons for refusal, which is commonly an unfavourable employment outlook in the field of activity and the geographic area concerned. Such a decision may be appealed if the reasons given are unjustified.

4.9   Holders of one-year residence permits should begin the re-application procedure two or three months before the current permit expires. At the time of re-application, the applicant must be able to prove adequate, stable financial resources, from a job or other sources.

COMMERICAL CARD (*Carte de Commercant*)

4.10   Non-EC nationals engaging in commerce or managing certain commercial or industrial activities in France, who do not hold a 10-year work and residence permit, must obtain a commercial card. They are also required to have a separate residence permit, which they can obtain with their commercial card.

Non-EC nationals who fall into the following categories must obtain a **4.11** commercial card: a shareholder in a Société en Nom Collectif (SNC); a shareholder with unlimited liability in a Société en Commandite Simple (SCS) or a Société en Commandite par Actions (SCA); a manager of a Société à Responsabité Limitée (SARL); a chairman of the board of directors of a Société Anonyme (SA); a president of the directorate or a managing director of an SA; a director authorised to conclude contracts with third parties on behalf of a Groupement d'Itérêt (GIE); a managing director of a branch or office of a foreign enterprise that carries out its activities in France; and a commercial agent.

Non-EC nationals living abroad must file an application for a commercial card with the nearest French consulate in their country of residence, and may file for a long-stay visa at the same time. Non-EC nationals who already hold a residence permit may file an application in France.

Treaties, exceptions and special regulations

France has signed treaties with the following countries that may favourably **4.12** affect nationals of those countries engaged in commercial activities in France: Central Africa, Congo, Gabon, Mali, Senegal, Switzerland, Togo, and the United States. Algerian nationals do not require a commercial card. Special regulations apply to running hairdressing salons and bars.

[*The next paragraph is 4.15.*]

(b) 10-year work and residence permit (*Carte de Résident*)

After three years of holding any type of temporary residence permit, EC and **4.15** non-EC nationals are eligible for a 10-year work and residence permit, which may be renewed automatically every ten years and authorises the holder to work anywhere in France, in any field of activity not specifically regulated by law (see para 4.20).

A combined work and residence permit may be *renewed* as a 10-year work and residence permit, since both permit the holder to work. The French authorities are reluctant to grant the 10-year permit to non-working residents, though substantial financial resources can tip the balance in the applicant's favour.

After 10 years of continuous legal residence in France, the authorities must **4.16** automatically grant the 10-year permit, unless the applicant has committed a crime serious enough to warrant his deportation (see paras 4.65–4.66).

A 10-year permit expires if the holder leaves France and does not re-enter for three consecutive years, though extensions may be granted under certain conditions.

The 10-year permit is granted automatically to certain categories of **4.17** residents, such as officially recognised refugees (see paras 4.61–4.64), parents of resident dependent French children, non-French children of French nationals, spouses of French nationals, and spouses and dependent family members of 10-year permit holders (see paras 4.25–4.44).

Favourable regulations apply to the nationals of the following countries with special relations to France: Andorra, Monaco, Central Africa, Togo, Gabon, Algeria, Tunisia, Cambodia, Laos, and Vietnam.

(c) Permit-free employment

4.18   Nationals of the European Community and the following countries are not required to obtain work permits: Andorra, Monaco, Central Africa, Gabon, and Togo.

4.19   Work permits are also unnecessary for non-French nationals in the following professional categories: diplomats, consuls and personnel of embassies and consulates; private servants of diplomats and consuls; personnel of international organisations who are not international administrative employees; ministers of religion; husbands/wives helping to run companies owned by a spouse; representatives of overseas newspapers, news agencies, or broadcasting organisations; personnel of transport companies in transit in France; crew members and navigators or pilots of ships or aircraft whose home port is overseas; private servants accompanying tourists (maximum stay of three months); resident representatives of overseas firms having no branch or subsidiary in France; and au pairs.

(d) Regulated professions

4.20   Special restrictions and/or regulations apply to the exercise of the following professions by non-French nationals: public administration employees (civil servants); teachers; medical and para-medical professionals; pharmacists; veterinarians; social workers; journalists; accountants and finance professionals; and professional athletes.

(ii) Persons of independent means/freelance workers – temporary residence permit: visitor status (*Carte de Séjour Temporaire: Statut Visiteur*)

(a) All non-French nationals

4.21   Non-working non-French nationals, such as retirees, persons of independent means, and non-French nationals working freelance in professions not requiring work permits (*e.g.*, translators, interpreters, artists, and writers) must obtain a "visitor" residence permit in order to stay in France for over three months. This permit is valid one year and is renewable.

4.22   Applicants must be able to prove that they have adequate financial resources to support themselves and their dependants without working, the minimum acceptable income being the net equivalent of the legal minimum wage (currently 5,000 FF per month) plus an additional amount (currently 2,400 FF per month) for each dependant.

Applicants must also show proof of insurance and adequate housing for themselves and their dependants.

(b) Non-EC nationals

Before departure, most non-EC nationals must obtain a long-stay visa from a　**4.23**
French consulate of their country of residence.

[*The next paragraph is 4.25.*]

(iii) **Family and marriage**

(a) General information

"Dependent family members" principally refers to dependent children under　**4.25**
18 (or 21 for certain nationals), and direct ascendents (parents and/or grandparents). This definition may be extended to include older children or other family members, provided they are financially dependent and/or continue to live under the same roof as the resident head-of-household.

The regulations concerning spouses and dependent family members who join or accompany resident non-French nationals depend on the nationality, residence status, and professional status of the non-French national, as well as the nationality of the spouse or dependent family member. Resident non-French nationals must provide written proof of the family relationship with their depandants (*i.e.* birth certificates).

The background of spouses or dependent family members from most　**4.26**
non-EC countries is subject to investigation through the International Migration Office (OMI) to verify that they present no danger to French law and order. The OMI also arranges for the obligatory medical examination for family members in the country of residence.

Residence permits for spouses and dependent family members usually　**4.27**
match that of the resident head-of-household with regard to the period of validity and authorisation to work. However, as non-EC residence permits are issued only for periods of one or ten years, spouses and dependent family members ineligible for EC permits are generally issued one-year permits, even if the head of household holds a five-year EC permit.

To give a few examples:
- The spouse of a non-French national who holds a 10-year work and residence permit is automatically eligible for the same permit.
- The EC spouse and dependent family members of an EC national who holds an EC residence permit are also eligible for EC permits.
- The non-EC spouse and dependent family members (over 16) of an EC national holding a five-year EC residence permit are eligible for renewable one-year work and residence permits. They become eligible, however, for a

10-year work and residence permit if the EC head-of-household obtains a 10-year EC residence permit upon renewal of his or her five-year permit (see paras 4.13–4.14).

– The spouse and dependent family members of a non-French national who holds a residence permit that does not permit employment are generally not granted work permits, unless they independently qualify for such permits.

(b) Spouses and dependent family members of non-French nationals

MARRIAGE

4.28 Non-French nationals holding a residence permit in France who marry non-French nationals in France may apply in France for a residence permits for their spouses. Adequate financial resources and housing and a medical examination are required.

NON-EC SPOUSES AND DEPENDENT FAMILY MEMBERS OF EC NATIONALS

4.29 Non-EC spouses and dependent family members who join or accompany an EC national to French for over three months must in most cases obtain a long-stay visa (*visa de long séjour*) before departure. Although some exceptions to this rule may be made for spouses and dependent family members of an EC head-of-household who is employed in France and intends to apply for an EC residence permit, it is more prudent to assume that the long-stay visa is obligatory, and to take the necessary steps to obtain it before departure from the country of residence.

To be accompanied by their families, non-working EC nationals must be able to prove adequate financial resources and suitable housing for themselves and all dependent family members (see para 4.24).

NON-EC SPOUSES AND DEPENDENT FAMILY MEMBERS OF NON-EC NATIONALS

4.30 Apart from the exceptions below, non-EC nationals must reside legally in France for at least one year before non-EC spouses and dependent family members are eligible to join them.

4.31 Executives may be permitted to forego the one-year waiting period through a so-called "accompanying family" (*famille accompagnante*) procedure under which the employer in France simultaneously submits the applications for the employee and the family while they are still abroad.

Exceptions to the above regulations apply to nationals of the following countries: Central Africa, Gabon, Burkina Faso, Mauritania, Togo and Algeria.

EC SPOUSES AND DEPENDENT FAMILY MEMBERS OF NON-FRENCH NATIONALS

4.32 EC spouses and dependent family members of resident non-French nationals may enter France without special permission, but must obtain a residence permit for stays of over three months. Non-working EC family members who accompany a non-working head-of-household will be granted one-year residence permits that do not permit employment. EC family members who wish to work are eligible to do so as EC nationals with an EC residence permit (see paras 4.13–4.14).

Adequate financial resources and housing must be proven for all dependent family members.

(c) Non-French spouses and dependent family members of French nationals

MARRIAGE

Many non-French nationals who come to France to be married to French **4.33** nationals within three months of entry may enter as tourists (see paras 4.56–4.57).

If the marriage will not take place within three months of arrival, most non-EC nationals must obtain a long-stay visa before leaving their country of residence (see paras 4.30–4.31).

SPOUSES AND DEPENDENT FAMILY MEMBERS

Spouses of French nationals are immediately and automatically eligible for the **4.34** 10-year work and residence permit. Non-French nationals residing in France before the marriage under a different type of work and/or residence permit may apply for the 10-year permit immediately after the marriage (see paras 4.15–4.17).

Non-French direct descendents and ascendents of French nationals or non-French spouses of French nationals are eligible to immigrate, provided they are dependent on the French national. Non-EC family members must obtain long-stay visas.

(d) Children

CHILDREN BORN IN FRANCE

Children born in France to non-French parents

Acquisition of French nationality is automatic for children who were born in **4.35** France to non-French parents, provided they habitually reside in France between the ages of 13 and 18, even if these children are already considered citizens of the country of origin of the parents. Such children should make their French nationality official by making a declaration before their eighteenth birthday. Before this declaration is made, however, a careful check of the laws of the country of origin of the parents regarding dual nationality should be performed to avoid possible inadvertent loss of the nationality of their parents origin.

Children born in France to at least one French parent, to unknown parents, or to stateless parents are automatically considered French nationals.

NON-FRENCH CHILDREN OF FRENCH NATIONALS

4.36   Before the age of 21, dependent non-French children of a French national are eligible for a 10-year work and residence permit, as are the financially dependent non-French ancestors and spouses of such children.

MINOR CHILDREN

4.37   Before the age of 18, dependent non-French children of legal residents are not required to hold a residence permit unless they intend to work. The minimum legal working age in France is 16. Children between the ages of 16 and 19 may normally obtain authorisation to work if one of their parents has a residence permit.

Non-EC children entering France are usually required to obtain a long-stay visa before leaving their country of residence (see paras 4.29–4.31).

Children of non-EC nationals

4.38   Children of non-EC nationals are normally considered dependents until the age of 18, although extensions may be granted if sufficient proof of continued dependence is provided (see paras 4.30–4.31).

[*The next paragraph is 4.40.*]

CHILDREN AGED 18 AND OVER

4.40   The ordinary 18-year age limit for dependent children is automatically extended to 21 years of age for children of EC nationals and nationals of the following countries: Austria, Cyprus, Iceland, Malta, Norway, Sweden and Turkey. The 18-year age limit may also be extended in other cases, provided the head of the family can produce sufficient proof of continued financial dependence.

4.41   All non-French children over the age of 18 must apply for a temporary residence permit within three months of arriving in France, or within the year after turning 18 in France. Dependent children will generally be granted residence permits valid for the same period as that of the head-of-household (see paras 4.25–4.27). Eligibility for work permits for dependent children between the ages of 19 and 21 depends on the nationality of the child, the situation of the child, and the type of work and residence permit of the head-of-household (see paras 4.25–4.27).

ADOPTED CHILDREN/CHILDREN RAISED IN FRANCE

Adopted children

4.42   Under French Law, plenary adoption, where all ties to the family of origin are severed, is distinguished from simple adoption, where ties to the family of origin are maintained. The attribution of French nationality is automatic for children adopted in a plenary adoption by a French national, or by a couple, if at least one member is a French national.

French nationality may be declared for children adopted in a simple adoption, provided they have been adopted by a French national, are under 18, and reside in France at the time of the declaration.

Children raised in France

French nationality may be declared for children raised by a French national or   **4.43**
by the French Social Services, and children who have received a French education for at least five years.

NON-FRENCH RELATIONS OF FRENCH CHILDREN

Non-French parents of a French child who lives in France are automatically   **4.44**
eligible for a 10-year work and residence permit, provided they have at least partial parental authority and/or financial responsibility for the child in question.

2. **Visitors, students and temporary workers**

(i) **Temporary workers**

Temporary workers are persons employed under contracts of less than one   **4.45**
year's duration.

(a) **Temporary non-EC workers – provisional work permit**
(*Autorisation Provisoire du Travail: APT*)

Non-EC nationals employed for less than one year are generally not eligible for   **4.46**
a combined work and residence permit, and must, therefore, obtain a provisional work permit, which is valid for a maximum of six months and may be renewed twice. This permit is available to employees who will be taking short-term employment in France and for permanent employees temporarily assigned to France by their employers.

Applications may be made in France, if the employee will be working for no   **4.47**
more than three months after legal entry into the country. For jobs lasting over three months, the applicant must obtain a long-stay visa from a French consulate abroad, for which a contract and a letter of invitation from the employer are required. Once in France, the employee must apply for a provisional work permit and a separate residence permit.

[*The next paragraph is 4.49.*]

(b) **Special regulations**
EXCEPTIONS ACCORDING TO PROFESSION

Special regulations apply to non-French nationals in the following professions: **4.49**
entertainers, language teachers, models, scientists, interpreters, farmers, bullfighters, and crew members of ships and aircraft. Special rules also apply to seasonal workers (contracts of six months or less), and border workers.

EXCEPTIONS FOR CERTAIN NATIONALS AND REFUGEES

Officially recognised refugees, EC nationals, and nationals of the following countries do not require a provisional work permit: Andorra, Monaco, Central Africa, Gabon, Monaco and Togo.

(ii) Trainees

4.50 A distinction is made between trainees of EC and non-EC nationality, and between professional and student trainees.

(a) Non-EC trainees

NON-EC PROFESSIONAL TRAINEES

4.51 Professionals between the ages of 18 and 21 (35 for the United States and Canada) from the following countries qualify for admission as professional trainees: Austria, Canada, Spain, the United States, Finland, Norway, New Zealand, Sweden, and Switzerland.

Non-EC professional trainees must apply from their country of residence, and are required to submit a work contract and a letter of invitation from the employer. Once approved, the contract may be used to obtain a long-stay visa. Once in France, the trainee will use the visa to obtain a provisional work permit valid for six months, with two possible six-month extensions, for a maximum total of 18 months. The trainee must also obtain a separate residence permit valid for one year (renewable) or for the period of the traineeship, whichever is shorter.

4.52 Trainee applicants without a contract may address the Office of International Migration (OMI) and the French National Employment Office (ANPE) for help in finding a prospective employer.

NON-EC STUDENT TRAINEES

4.53 A long-stay visa is required for non-EC students in traineeships lasting over three months and the students must prove that the traineeship is part of their course of studies. Student trainees will be granted a provisional work permit (APT) valid for a maximum of six months with possible extensions according to the length of the traineeship (see paras 4.46–4.47).

[*The next paragraph is 4.56.*]

(iii) Students

(a) Non-EC students

4.56 Non-EC students must apply for a long-stay visa from a French consulate in their country of residence abroad, for which they must have an immatriculation or pre-immatriculation certificate from an accredited French university or other institution of higher education (most French language schools do not qualify). Applicants are required to show sufficient financial resources to support themselves without working, as well as health insurance and the results of a medical examination by a consulate-approved doctor. Once in France, students must apply for a student residence permit, which is valid for one year and renewable.

STUDENT WORK PERMITS

Undergraduates enrolled in their second consecutive academic year in a **4.57** French university or other institution of higher education, and graduate students enrolled in their first academic year are generally eligible to work during school vacations with a provisional work permit (see paras 4.46–4.47).

To be granted a provisional work permit at other times in the academic year, non-EC students must justify the unexpected and involuntary disappearance of the financial resources used to obtain their long-stay visa (*e.g.* cutting-off of scholarship funds). Decisions are made on a case-by-case basis.

[*The next paragraph is 4.59.*]

(b) Students in medicine, dentistry and pharmacy

Work permits are not required after the first academic year for non-French **4.59** students in French medical, dentistry, or pharmacy schools where work in hospitals or clinics is an integral part of the curriculum, nor for interns covered by intergovernmental treaties.

(c) Spouses and children of students

NON-EC STUDENTS

Most non-EC students must hold a residence permit for at least one year before **4.60** their spouse and/or dependent children will be allowed to join them (see paras 4.30–4.31). The spouse and dependent family members of resident students are normally granted one-year residence permits that do not permit employment, but are eligible to work if the student holds a provisional work permit.

[*The next paragraph is 4.62.*]

(iv) **Au pairs/family helpers**

(a) General information

Au pairs, or "family helpers" must be between 18 and 30, be enrolled in a **4.62** French language course, and have a signed "placement" contract for 3 to 12 months (with a possible extension to 18 months) with a resident host family.

Au pairs may work no more than five hours per day, must be given at least one full day off per week (which must include at least one Sunday per month), and be paid between 75–90% of the hourly legal minimum wage. The host family must declare au pairs to the social security authorities, and pay the obligatory social security premiums.

(b) Non-EC au pairs

4.63   The host family must apply to have the placement contract authorised by the French labour authorities. If the prospective au pair does not already hold a residence permit, the application must be submitted when he or she is still abroad.

Since au pairs are also students, the procedure for obtaining a long-stay visa and residence card is very similar to that for ordinary students. Once in France, au pairs must apply for a student residence permit, and will be granted a provisional work permit with the placement contract and the student residence permit. Nationals of certain non-EC countries do not require a provisional work permit (see paras 4.46–4.47).

[*The next paragraph is 4.65.*]

(v) **Short-term visitors**

4.65   Short-term visitors are defined as tourists, business visitors and private visitors in transit or seeking temporary residence in France (three months or less) for specific purposes.

Entry may be refused to visitors if there is reason to doubt the authenticity of the required documents or to suspect fraudulent intentions of the visitor; if the visitor is deemed to endanger French law and order; if the visitor has been the subject of a deportation decision; or if the visitor has been legally barred from entering French territory.

(a) Tourists

4.66   No visa is necessary for visits of three months or less by nationals of the following countries: Andorra, Austria, Belgium, Canada, Cyprus, Czechoslavakia, Denmark, Finland, Germany, Great Britain, Greece, Holland, Hungary, Iceland, Ireland, Italy, Japan, Liechtenstein, Luxembourg, Malta, Monaco, Norway, Portugal, Saint-Marin, South Korea, Spain, Sweden, Switzerland, the United States, and the Vatican. Short-stay visas are required for other nationals visiting for less than three months.

4.67   All tourists must have a valid passport (or ID card, for EC tourists) and may be asked to produce proof of the touristic nature of their visit, such as a return ticket, proof of hotel accommodation, proof of health insurance, and proof of financial resources for the trip (*e.g.*, cash, international credit cards, or travellers' checks). In rare cases, financial deposits or guarantees concerning the return trip may be asked of overland travellers with no return-trip ticket.

(b) Business visitors

4.68   In addition to short-stay visas (where applicable), non-EC nationals on business trips to France lasting three months or less must be able to show proof of financial means, their professional activity, and the reason for their visit to France (*e.g.*, letters of invitation from or related correspondence with a French company or organisation). They are expected to be in possession of a round-trip ticket.

Non-EC business visitors planning to stay over three months must apply for a provisional work permit: (see paras 4.46–4.47).

(c) **Private visitors** – **certificate of accommodation** (*Certificat d'Hébergement*)

In addition to short-stay visas (where applicable), return-trip guarantees, and insurance, non-EC nationals who intend to visit resident friends or family must obtain from them a certificate of accommodation. This certificate, which must be approved by the local town hall of the resident host, specifies the visitor, the resident host, and the family relationship between the two (where applicable); the date and the place of delivery of the residence permit (non-French nationals) or the identity card (French nationals) of the resident host; and the housing conditions (i.e. general lay-out and surface area per inhabitant). **4.69**

(d) **Exceptions**

The above requirements are not applicable to short-term visitors who are: EC nationals; Swiss nationals; spouses and dependent children coming to reside with a resident head-of-household (see paras 4.29–4.31); talented or skilled persons capable of providing valuable services to France; persons involved in recognised charitable activities in France; persons given special dispensation from a French consulate in their home country; members of diplomatic or consular missions on official business in France and their dependent family members; members of foreign parliamentary assemblies; officials or agents of intergovernmental organisations to which France is party on official business in France; officers and agents of a foreign government or civil service on official business in France; and crew members of ships and aircraft on business covered by international treaties. **4.70**

3. **Refugees and political asylum**

(i) **Refugees**

In accordance with international treaty, persons seeking official refugee status in France who arrive from a third country where they could have applied for refugee status will generally be compelled to return and apply for asylum there. **4.71**

Asylum-seekers should apply for refugee status without delay upon arrival in France, since the requests of aliens who have entered France illegally are usually refused. Applicants will be given a provisional work and residence permit until a final decision has been made on their case by the French Office for the Protection of Refugees and Stateless Persons (OFPRA).

If refugee status is granted, the applicant will automatically be granted a 10-year work and residence permit (see paras 4.15–4.17).

(ii) Stateless persons

4.72 Stateless persons officially recognised as such by the OFPRA are eligible for a temporary work and residence permit. Persons who hold this permit for three years will automatically be granted a 10-year work and residence permit (see paras 4.15–4.17).

4. Permanent residence and nationality

4.73 Direct ancestors and descendents of French nationals are normally eligible for naturalisation by declaration (see paras 4.25–4.44).

The spouse of a French national may apply for naturalisation as a French citizen at any time after six months of marriage, if the couple continues to live together. Dual nationality is accepted under French law, but the applicant should verify the laws of his or her country of origin. While waiting for naturalisation, the spouse is eligible for a 10-year work and residence permit.

4.74 Other non-French nationals must prove that they are well-integrated into French society, notably in terms of sufficient knowledge of the French language, and must be considered persons of good moral standing, who have not been convicted of a crime or misdemeanour in France.

Non-French nationals over 18 are ordinarily eligible to apply for French nationality by decree after five years of continuous residence in France. This waiting period may be reduced to two years for talented or skilled persons who have provided, or are capable of providing, valuable services to France, and for persons who have successfully completed two years of higher education in France.

5. Sanctions

(i) Deportation

4.75 Persons who fall into the following categories may be subject to deportation: persons unable to prove legal entry and/or residence in France; persons continuing to reside in France for more than one month after a refusal to grant or renew a residence permit; persons barred from entering French territory; persons considered to endanger French law and order; and persons convicted of forgery, falsification of documents, counterfeiting, or entering or residing in France under an assumed name.

Notwithstanding the above, certain categories of residents are not subject to **4.76** deportation under specified conditions.

Judges may use considerable discretion in a deportation decision, and take into account not only the infraction in question, but also the circumstances and the personal background of the offender.

(ii) **Illegal entry**

Non-French nationals who illegally enter or reside in France are subject to **4.77** varying fines and terms of imprisonment, and may be barred from entering French territory for specified periods.

(iii) **Detention**

Persons who have been refused entry into France have the right to request to **4.78** stay for up to 24 hours in a non-prison detention facility in order to contact their consulate, legal council, or persons expecting them in France.

All persons suspected of having committed crimes in France are generally subject to be held for 48 hours for questioning in a non-prison facility without being formally charged. Persons held for illegal entry or residence will be notified of a deportation decision during this period, and are held for an additional 24 hours to give time for appeal, in which case detention may be extended until the appellate court's decision is rendered (six days maximum).

6. **Tax and social considerations**

(i) **Tax considerations**

Persons who are tax residents are subject to French tax on their world-wide **4.79** income and careful tax planning is advised for well-compensated employees and persons with significant assets. Persons falling into the following categories are considered residents for tax purposes: persons whose permanent home is in France; persons who spend more than 183 days in a calendar year in France; persons who exercise professional activities in France; and persons for whom France is the centre of their economic interest. Persons earning income for services performed in France are generally subject to tax on that income. Similarly, income derived from real estate is generally taxable in France.

France has treaties with many countries which eliminate or reduce double taxation.

(ii) **Social considerations**

Complex social security regulations and regulations concerning other social **4.80** benefits vary according to the individual situation, and are, therefore, beyond the scope of this chapter.

It should be noted, however, that social security payments represent a very significant part of the total tax burden on earned income. Under treaties with certain countries, an employee who is transferred to France for five years or less may elect to continue to pay social security taxes in his or her home country and be excused from French social security taxes.

Germany

Chapter 5
Germany[1]

Introduction

Except in certain specified circumstances, individuals seeking entry into **5.1** Germany must obtain a residence permit and if they seek to work while in Germany, they must obtain a work permit.

German immigration law is covered by several statutes, directives and **5.2** regulations. The most important statute is the Foreigners Act or *Ausländergesetz* of 9 July 1990 with its directive (*Verordnung zur Durchführung des Ausländergesetzes* of 18 December 1990). EC nationals, however, are separately treated by the EC Residency Act (*Aufenthaltsgesetz/EWG*) of 31 January 1980, as amended in 1981 and 1990. Work permits are regulated by section 19 of the Law to Promote Employment (*Arbeitsförderungsgesetz*) of 25 June 1969 as amended 1991 and the Work Permit Directive or *Arbeitserlaubnisverordnung* of 12 September 1980 as amended 1990. Asylum is separately covered by the Act on the Rules of Procedure for Asylum (*Asylverfahrensgesetz*) of 9 April 1991.

All persons intent on doing business in or visiting Germany must check **5.3** whether she or he is required to apply for a residence permit (*Aufenthaltsgenehmigung*) and a work permit (*Arbeitserlaubnis*). Additional issues of asylum and taxes and social security also arise.

1. **Residence permit** (*Aufenthaltsgenehmigung*)

In general, German immigration law requires that each foreign national **5.4** seeking entry into Germany must apply for a residence permit. There are, however, certain practical and important exceptions to this general requirement.

(i) **Exceptions**

Three general categories of foreign nationals are exempt from the requirement **5.5** of a residency permit.

(a) **Tourists**

Tourists, as defined in section 1 of the Foreigners Act Directive, are nationals of **5.6** the countries listed in Annex I (see the Appendix at the end of this chapter) of

---

[1] The author wishes to acknowledge the assistance of Peter D. Guattery of Whiteford, Taylor & Preston, Baltimore, Maryland, USA, in the preparation of this chapter.

the Foreigners Act Directive provided:
- Their stay in Germany does not exceed three months; and
- they have a passport or other identification document that according to bi- or multi-lateral agreements allows visa-free entry; and
- they are not working.

[*The next paragraph is 5.8.*]

(b) Others (ss 2–8 Foreigners Act Directive)

5.8　Sections 2–8 of the Foreigners Act Directive also provide for the following miscellaneous exceptions:

(i)　children under 16 of EC or EFTA countries, or from (the former territory of) Yugoslavia, Morocco, Turkey or Tunisia if they meet certain other requirements;

(ii)　members of foreign consulates or embassies;

(iii)　nationals with special passports such as EC Parliamentarians;

(iv)　nationals of countries listed in Annex II (see the Appendix at the end of this chapter) of the Foreigners Act Directive provided that they hold passports of the kind mentioned in Annex II;

(v)　as may be provided for in bi- or multi-lateral agreements;

(vi)　nationals of certain neighbouring territories and in cases of emergency;

(vii)　flight personnel and passengers if they meet certain requirements; special provisions apply for passengers from countries listed in Annex III (see the Appendix at the end of this chapter) of the Foreigners Act Directive;

(viii)　crew and passengers on ships and pilots if they meet certain requirements.

(ii) Individuals requiring a residence permit

5.9　If an individual does not meet any of the above exceptions, he or she must apply for a residence permit.

(a) Right of residence

5.10　Certain classes of individuals are entitled to receive a residence permit and the competent authorities have no discretion in deciding whether to grant the permit or not (s 6 I Foreigners Act):

(i)　EC and EFTA nationals according to the EC Residency Act;

(ii)　individuals recognised as having a right of asylum;

(iii)　foreign nationals over the age of 15 but under the age of 21, provided they grew up in Germany and meet certain minimum residency and financial support requirements;

(iv)　spouse, children and other relatives of foreign nationals if the foreign national living in Germany meets certain requirements (ss 17–22 Foreigners Act);

(v) foreign spouses, children and parents of a German national domiciled in Germany (s 23 Foreigners Act);

(vi) foreign nationals who have lived and worked in Germany for an extended period of time (*e.g.* 8 years) including their spouses and children if certain other requirements are met (ss 24–27 Foreigners Act).

(b) Discretionary permits

In all cases where the applicant has no entitlement to a residence permit, the competent Foreigners' Office is permitted the exercise of considerable discretion (s 7 I Foreigners Act) in the grant or denial of a residence permit. Predicting when a residence permit may be granted in such circumstances is thus extremely difficult. The availability of a residence permit instead depends upon the specific circumstances of each individual case. **5.11**

The Foreigners Act only stipulates when the residence permit is to be refused. **5.12**

(i) The residence permit, other than in exceptional circumstances, will be refused (s 7 II Foreigners Act) if:
    – there is reason for explulsion or *Ausweisung* (s 45 Foreigners Act);
    – the foreign national cannot pay for his maintenance;
    – German public policy may be impaired or jeopardised if residence is permitted.

(ii) The residence permit will always be refused (s 8 Foreigners Act), if:
    – the foreign national
        • entered Germany without the required visa;
        • entered Germany with a visa which due to the information provided by the applicant was granted without the necessary consent of the foreigners' office;
        • has no required passport; or
    – the identity or nationality is unknown and he has no right to return to another country.

(c) Types of residence permits

There are six different types of residence permits (s 5 Foreigners Act, s 1 IV EC Residency Act, s 20 Act on the Rules of Procedure for Asylum). The names of the different residence permits are basically descriptive terms and so is the translation. **5.13**

RESIDENCE LEAVE (*Aufenthaltserlaubnis*)

When the foreign national's stay is permitted without any restriction as to its purpose, the residence permit will be granted as a residence leave (s 15 Foreigners Act). In general, however, a residence leave will only be granted for a limited period of time. **5.14**

A residence leave should be applied for if foreign nationals intend to work in Germany for an extended period of time or if they want to apply for a residence permit for their family members.

5.15   The work Residency Directive (*Arbeitsaufenthalteverordnung*) of 18 December 1990 permits a residence leave to be granted in the following circumstances:

5.16   (i)   Residence leave with time limit:
- for the duration of the employment of domestic servants of a diplomatic or consular representative;
- for not more than five years: school and university language teachers meeting specified requirements;
- for not more than three years: highly qualified cooks.

5.17   (ii)   Residence leave for duration of specified employment for:
- highly qualified scientists for employment in research and teaching where such employment is in the public interest;
- highly qualified specialists with a university or other comparable degree where such employment is in the public interest;
- executives and specialists employed with a business located in Germany, having its principal place of business in the home country of the executives or specialists (note: an important factor in determining whether an applicant is "specialist" is whether he has special knowledge or information which is peculiar to the business he is employed by);
- executives in a German–foreign joint-venture established in conformity with the terms of a bilateral treaty;
- skilled individuals engaged in social work for foreign nationals and their families provided the individuals are sufficiently proficient in the German language;
- pastors meeting certain specified requirements;
- members of religious orders meeting certain specified requirements;
- nurses meeting certain minimum qualifications. Nurses from European countries enjoy preferential status;
- artists including their support personnel;
- professional sportsmen and trainers employed by German clubs and who meet certain eligibility requirements.

5.18   (iii)   Section 24 of the Foreigners Act permits residence leave to be extended without time limit if the applicant:
- has had a residence leave for the past five years (No. 1);
- is an employee and has a special work permit (see paras 5.43–5.44) (No. 2);
- has all other required permits for permanently conducting his occupation (No. 3);
- has a basic ability to communicate in German (No. 4);
- has sufficient housing available for himself and any dependents if living together (No. 5); and
- gave no reason for expulsion.

[The next paragraph is 5.20.]

RESIDENCE ENTITLEMENT (*Aufenthaltsberechtigung*)

A residence permit is granted as a residence entitlement (s 27 Foreigners Act) **5.20** only if the foreign national, after a period of time, usually eight years, has adapted to German society and has adequate maintenance and housing available. Residence entitlement is not limited in time or by geographic area.

RESIDENCE APPROVAL (*Aufenthaltsbewilligung*)

A residence permit will be granted as a residence approval if the stay is for a **5.21** definite and temporary purpose (s 28 I Foreigners Act). A residence approval may be granted for only two years, and may only be extended in certain defined circumstances.

The Work Residency Directive (*Arbeitsaufenthalteverordnung*) of 18 December 1990 permits residence approval in the following circumstances:

(i)   Residence approval for educational purposes: **5.22**
  – graduates of German or foreign universities or other trainees to be mainly employed for further training in German universities or other institutions licensed for such training.

(ii) Residence approval for educational purposes with a two-year time limit: **5.23**
  – university graduates seeking practical work experience in area of training;
  – skilled individuals and executives working in German businesses or commercial associations in accordance with the provisions of bi- or multi-lateral treaties or certain other agreements.

(iii) Residence approval for educational purposes with an 18 months' time **5.24** limit:
  – guest workers for professional and language training in accordance with bi- or multi-lateral treaties;
  – foreign nationals temporarily employed by a German business partner with the purpose of being introduced to business practices or work methods.

(iv) Residence approval for educational purposes with a one-year time limit: **5.25**
  – foreign nationals in a temporary training programme in Germany or who are in Germany in order to carry out an export or licensing contract;
  – foreign nationals under the age of 25 years engaged in au pair employment.

(v)   Residence approval for employees for contracts for work and services: **5.26**
  – employees who are working to fulfill contracts for work and services may be granted a residence approval under certain circumstances.

RESIDENCE AUTHORITY (*Aufenthaltsbefugnis*)

Residence authority may be granted if the requirements for a residence leave **5.27** (*Aufenthaltserlaubnis*) are not met, but the applicant shall have a right to stay due to humanitarian, public international law or political reasons.

RESIDENCE ALLOWANCE (*Aufenthaltsgestattung*)

5.28   Residence allowance is a very restricted residence permit and will by law be effected by an application for asylum (s 20 Act on the Rules of Procedure for Asylum (*Asylverfahrensgesetz*)), (see paras 5.52–5.54).

(iii) Time

5.29   In general an application for a residence permit must be filed with the competent authorities *before* entry into Germany. It is not permissible, for example, to enter Germany as a tourist and then apply for a residence permit (ss 8 I, 71 I 2 Foreigners Act).

    There are certain important exceptions to the above rule: EC and EFTA nationals and US citizens are allowed to apply for a residence permit after entering Germany.

(iv) Competent authorities

5.30   In general, an application for a residence permit is to be filed with an authorised German consulate or embassy in the applicant's home country (s 63 III Foreigners Act). If the applicant intends to work or stay more than three months in Germany the consent of the local Foreigner's Office (*Ausländerbehörde*) of the applicant's intended place of residence is required.

    If the application is filed after entry into Germany, it must be filed with the Foreigner's Office having jurisdiction over the applicant's actual place of residence.

(v) Remedies

5.31   If the applicant is not satisfied with the decision of the Foreigners' Office or any other competent authority he may file a formal objection (*Widerspruch*) to the particular decision (ss 68 *et seq* Rules of Procedure of the Administrative Courts or *Verwaltungsgerichtsordnung*). The *Widerspruch* will then be considered and ruled on.

5.32   If the applicant remains unsatisfied with the agency's decision the applicant may institute legal proceedings before the competent Administrative Court (*Verwaltungsgericht*) to overturn the decision.

2. Work permit (*Arbeitserlaubnis*)

5.33   According to section 19 of the Law to Promote Employment (*Arbeitsförderungsgesetz*) of 25 June 1969 (as amended 1991) every foreign national who wants to work in Germany needs a work permit. The permit will be granted, dependent upon the situation of the labour market and the particular circumstances of each individual case.

The Work Permit Directive (*Arbeitserlaubnisverordnung*) of 12 September 1980 (as amended 1990) was enacted in order to advise the competent authorities on how to apply the vague language of this provision.

A residence permit (see paras 5.4–5.32) needs to be applied for before the application for a work permit can be made. According to section 5 of the Work Permit Directive, a work permit will only be granted to foreign nationals who legally reside in Germany. Thus, in general, a work permit will be issued only if a residence permit has been previously granted. Furthermore, the work permit will automatically become null and void if the residence permit should become invalid (s 8 I No. 1, Work Permit Directive). **5.34**

(i) Exceptions

A work permit is generally required for all employment. However, if a person is self-employed, a work permit is not required. Moreover, the employment must be for a consideration in the form of wages or at least typically be expected to be for payment. A foreigner is permitted to perform volunteer work without a work permit. **5.35**

A work permit is necessary notwithstanding the nature of employment, its duration, or otherwise provided prior permission or qualification is obtained to perform certain services (*e.g.* for physicians). **5.36**

The following list of examples details the most relevant cases where (ii) a work permit is necessary or (iii) where a work permit is unnecessary.

(ii) Work permit required

A work permit is required in the following cases: **5.37**
(i)   for household work and childcare if done for payment and if the salary is not paid in compliance with an obligation to provide maintenance;
(ii)   for vocational industrial or other similar training;
(iii)   for nursing staff, including trainees;
(iv)   for au pair employment;
(v)   for models if not self-employed;
(vi)   for certain visiting physicians if a permit according to a German statute regulating medical practice is required;
(vii)   for fraternal workers.

(iii) Work permit not required

(a) S 9 Work Permit Directive

According to section 9 Work Permit Directive a work permit is not required in the following cases: **5.38**
(i)   individuals referred to in section 5 II Works Constitution Act (*Betriebsverfassungsgesetz*), *i.e.* individuals not regarded as employees, and executives who have been granted general power of attorney (*Generalvollmacht*) or full power of attorney (*Prokura*);

(ii)   certain employees engaged in the international carriage of goods and passengers and with certain exceptions the staff of vessels and aircraft;

(iii)   foreign nationals who remain domiciled in a foreign country and who are sent by their employer to Germany in order to:
- do erection or maintenance work or repairs for plants or machines;
- to inspect plants, machines or other goods for acceptance or to provide instruction on the use of said machines or goods;
- to complete company training in the course of export, delivery, and licensing agreements;

(iv)   foreign nationals who come for a speech or other presentation of particular scientific or artistic value or for sports events, for a period not to exceed three months;

(v)   foreign speakers who offer only daily presentations on an irregular and non-permanent basis:

(vi)   professors and certain other members of the scientific staff and university assistants if certain further requirements are met;

(vii)   school children and students at universities for a temporary employment of not more than two months per year and school children and students for vacation jobs;

(viii) individuals working in consular or diplomatic missions or with international organisations;

(ix)   journalists, correspondents and reporters if accredited by the Press and Information Office of the Federal Government;

(x)   professional sportspersons;

(xi)   individuals falling under the NATO Status of Forces Agreement (*NATO-Truppenstatut*);

(xii)   individuals employed by a German employer as commercial employees in a foreign country, who in the course of their employment work in Germany for a period not to exceed three months;

(xiii) individuals who have been granted a residence authority (s 27 Foreigners Act).

(b) Other cases

5.39 Although section 9 of the Work Permit Directive sets forth the exemptions in detail, there are some relevant border line cases:

(i)   a work permit is not required for the practical education of pharmacy and medicine students if necessary to their studies in Germany;

(ii)   a work permit is not required for foreign nationals receiving practical training in judicial or other legal work in Germany after having passed the first German state examination (*Rechtsreferendare*);

(iii)   a work permit is not required for foreign physicians if not practising in Germany, particularly physicians whose stay is brief (days or weeks) for a congress or for further education;

(iv)   concert soloists are not required to apply for a work permit. Other musicians are exempt from applying for a work permit only if they play at purely private events or solely for their private entertainment;

(v) a work permit is not required for radio presentations if the foreign national is economically and socially independent from the radio station. A freelance worker under certain circumstances, however, may be an "employee" for work permit purposes.

(iv) **Types of work permit**

There are two types of work permit: (i) a general, and (ii) a special work **5.40** permit. The special work permit is usually applied for only after a general work permit has been issued.

(a) General Work Permit

The general work permit will be granted where the current and future needs of **5.41** the employment market, considered, with the circumstances of the individual case, so allow (s 19 I 2 Law on the Promotion of Employment, s 1 I Work Permit Directive).

Although the "circumstances of the individual case" must be considered, a work permit generally will be denied in industrial centres and in unfavourable economic situations.

Where the application is made to renew a work permit, the requirements of **5.42** section 19 I 2 of the Law on the Promotion of Employment must also be fulfilled. In general, a foreign national who has already received a work permit will be granted a renewal if his employer can establish that he wants to further employ this employee in Germany for business reasons in accordance with section 19 I 2 of the Law on the Promotion of Employment.

Typically a general work permit is only valid for employment within the district of the local employment office (s 3 I Work Permit Directive).

The general work permit will be granted for the time of the employment only and its maximum duration will be limited to three years (s 4 I Work Permit Directive).

(b) Special work permit

A special work permit will be granted in accordance with section 19 VI of the **5.43** Law on the Promotion of Employment and section 2 Work Permit Directive. A special work permit is normally sought after a longer period of integration of a foreign national.

In general, a special work permit is valid for employment within Germany without any geographical restriction (s 3 II Work Permit Directive). In certain exceptional cases, however, a geographical restriction may be imposed.

A special work permit is typically granted without any time limit (s 19 VI **5.44** Law on the Promotion of Employment, however, *cf.* for time limits s 4 Work Permit Directive).

The prerequisites for a special work permit are independent of the present state and future development of the employment market and in particular a special work permit will be granted in the following cases.

SECTION 19 VI LAW ON THE PROMOTION OF EMPLOYMENT

5.45   A special work permit will be granted to a foreign employee if within the eight years preceding the validity of the special work permit he or she lawfully worked for a total period of five years in Germany. "Lawfully" in this context denotes that said employee had a valid general work permit during this time period.

5.46   In calculating the five year time period, the following periods of work will not be considered:

(i)   work performed by the employee in Germany in order to fulfill an agreement for work and services concluded between his foreign employer and a German enterprise;

(ii)   work performed during the time period the employee was, due to the Work Permit Directive or due to an international treaty, exempt from applying for a work permit;

(iii)   work performed by the employee prior to leaving Germany and giving up his ordinary residence (*gewöhnlicher Aufenthalt*) in Germany;

(iv)   work which prepares the employee for an occupation abroad;

(v)   work for which no contribution to the Federal Employment Office is required according to section 169a of the Law on the Promotion of Employment (*i.e.* short-term employment with a weekly working time of less than 18 hours, s 102 Law on the Promotion of Employment).

SECTION 2 WORK PERMIT DIRECTIVE

5.47   (i)   If a foreign national lives together with a German member of his family and has been granted a residence leave according to section 23 I of the Foreigners Act.

(ii)   If a foreign national has been recognised as having a right to asylum.

(iii)   If a foreign national has a valid passport for refugees issued by a German authority.

(iv)   Certain refugees according to a special act on humanitarian support of 22 July 1980 as amended in 1990.

(v)   A foreign national who has been "taken over" according to section 33 Foreigners Act and who has been granted a residence authority.

(vi)   A foreign national who has been in Germany for six years and who has been granted a residence leave or residence authority (ss 15, 17 or 30 Foreigners Act).

(vii)   A foreign national who has been granted a residence leave or residence authority (ss 15, 17 or 30 Foreigners Act) if he came to Germany under the age of 18 and graduated here from an accredited secondary school or received an education in an officially accredited or comparably regulated vocational training programme, participated in a special practical training programme or concluded a contract of apprenticeship in an officially accredited apprenticeship trade.

(viii)   A foreign national who has been granted a residence leave according to section 16 I or II Foreigners law.

(ix)   If, under the individual circumstances, a denial of the work permit
        would be an undue hardship to the foreign national.

In so far as the foreign national is required to stay in Germany for a certain   **5.48**
period of time (see para 5.47 (vi)), a temporary absence of up to six months will
not interrupt the time periods required for a work permit.

(v) Time

Application for a work permit must be made prior to the commencement of   **5.49**
employment or before expiration of an existing work permit.

Due to section 5 of the Work Permit Directive, an application for a work
permit is without success and, therefore, an application should not be filed,
before the applicant has been granted a residence permit.

(vi) Competent authorities

Under section 11 of the Work Permit Directive, the foreign national must file a   **5.50**
written application with the local employment office or *Arbeitsamt*. The
employment office having jurisdiction over the application is the employment
office at the place of employment of the applicant. The place of employment is
the place of business of the factory or establishment. If the place where the
employee works constantly changes, the place of employment is at the place of
business where payroll accounting is performed.

(vii) Remedies

If not satisfied with the decision of the local employment office, the applicant   **5.51**
can make a formal objection (*Widerspruch*) against the particular decision (ss
78 *et seq* Social Courts Act or *Sozialgerichtsgesetz*).

If he should not be satisfied with any subsequent decision, the applicant may
then institute legal proceedings before the competent Social Court (*Sozial-
gericht*).

3. Refugees and political asylum

The German constitution (Basic Law or *Grundgesetz*) in art 16 II 2   **5.52**
unequivocally provides that: "Persons persecuted for political reasons enjoy
the right of asylum."

Asylum is regulated by the Act on the Rules of Procedure for Asylum
(*Asylverfahrensgesetz*). According to section 20 of this statute, by operation of
law the application for asylum permits the applicant a residence allowance
(see para 5.28). Thus the applicant is allowed to stay in Germany during the
time period in which his application is pending.

Although the term "political asylum" is not defined by the statute, the   **5.53**
German courts have provided guidance for its interpretation. In general, the
inquiry will focus on the question of whether the reason for the persecution of
the applicant is "political". "Political" has been defined very narrowly and

does not include a mere criminal persecution. Economic reasons for a residence in Germany will also not be taken into account by the competent authorities.

A foreign national has no right of asylum if he previously obtained safe leave from political persecution in a different country, or the reason for political persecution has been created after entry into Germany.

5.54 Applicants with a right of asylum enjoy the status of a refugee according to the Convention of the Status of Refugees of 28 July 1951.

The application for asylum may be filed after entry into Germany. The application may be refused and entry into Germany denied only if it is obviously without merit.

Thus, the Law of Asylum is under much reconsideration and discussion and a change in the constitution might be expected in the near future. The heavy influx of asylum seekers and the political and social problems related thereto in recent years, have provoked a strong consensus for reconsideration of Germany's asylum law.

4. Nationality

5.55 The general statute regulating naturalisation of foreign nationals is the *Reich-Citizen* and Nationality Act or *Reichs- und Staatsangehörigkeitsgesetz* of 22 July 1913 (as amended 1986). Some foreign nationals, however, are privileged if they meet the requirements of ss 85 *et seq* Foreigners Act.

(i) Section 85 *et seq* Foreigners Act

(a) Privileged naturalisation of young aliens

5.56 A foreign national over the age of 16 but under the age of 23 at the time of application may be naturalised, if he or she:
- renounces or loses his nationality (some exceptions may be made with respect to this requirement under s 87 Foreigners Act);
- has had a lawful primary residence in Germany for eight years;
- attended school in Germany for six years, four years of which were at a secondary school (*allgemeinbildende Schule*); and
- has not been convicted of a crime.

(b) Privileged naturalisation of aliens with long residence

5.57 A foreign national who has lawfully resided in Germany for 15 years and has applied for naturalisation by 31 December 1995 will be naturalised in accordance with section 86 Foreigners Act, if he or she:
- renounces or loses his nationality (some exceptions are made with respect to this requirement under s 87 Foreigners Act),
- has not been convicted of a crime, and
- can pay his own and his dependants' living expenses without utilising state welfare benefits or unemployment relief; if the applicant is not able to meet such living expenses through no fault of his own, the authorities might dispense with this requirement.

(ii) General requirements for naturalisation

According to section 8 of the *Reich-Citizen* and Nationality Act a foreign   **5.58**
national, residing in Germany, may, upon application, be naturalised by the
state he is residing in, if he:
- has acquired legal capacity according to the laws of his former home
  country, if he would have acquired legal capacity according to German
  law, or if his application is filed according to section 7 II 2 of the Act by his
  legal representative or with the consent of his legal representative;
- has conducted a "respectable way of life" (*unbescholtenen Lebenswandel*);
- maintains his own residence; and
- is in a position to maintain himself and his dependants at this place of
  residence.

5. Tax and social security considerations

Foreign nationals who come to Germany are required to pay German income   **5.59**
tax and contribute to German social security insurance funds. Although a
detailed survey of such laws is beyond the scope of this study, some practical
and useful guide-lines should be taken into consideration, such as tax and
social security insurance rates.

(i) Income tax

German law requires that the employer deduct the employee's income tax   **5.60**
from the employee's monthly salary.

    There is no flat income tax rate. Rather, the income tax rate rises as salary   **5.61**
increases. Although the actual calculation of the income tax is complex, a basic
formula (s 32a Income Tax Act) may serve as a rough guide:

Annual Income (DM)	*Calculation*
up to 5,616.00	no income tax
5,617.00–8,153.00	$0.19x - 1,067$
8,154.00–120,041.00	$y(151.94y + 1,900) + 472$
over 120,042.00	$0.53x - 22,842$

x is defined as the rounded down taxable income.
y is defined as a ten thousandth of the rounded down taxable income exceeding
DM 8,100.00.

(ii) Social security

There are three general types of mandatory social security insurance in   **5.62**
Germany: health insurance, unemployment insurance, and pension insurance.

    Only employees are required to contribute to these social security insurance funds. Self-employed foreign nationals are not required to contribute.

5.63   If the employee's monthly salary exceeds DM 6,800.00 (as of August 1992) he is also exempt from the requirement to contribute to the unemployment and pension insurances. If the employee's salary exceeds DM 5,100.00 he is exempt from contributing to health insurance.

As of August 1992 the social security insurance rates as a percentage of gross income are as follows:

Health Insurance	13.1%
Unemployment Insurance	6.3%
Pension Insurance	17.7%

5.64   Health insurance rates vary slightly from these rates depending upon the insurance company. All insurance companies within the social security insurances are publicly controlled and limited in number. Private insurance companies exist only for individuals exempt from the requirement to contribute to the mandatory health insurance.

Appendix – Visa exemptions
Annex I Foreigners Act Directive

A5.1

Andorra
Argentina
Australia
   as well as the Coconut Islands,
   the Norfolk Islands,
   Christmas Island
Austria

Belgium
Benin
Bolivia
Brazil
Brunei
Burkina Faso

Canada
Chile
Colombia
Costa Rica
Cyprus
Czech Republic

Denmark

Ecuador
El Salvador

Finland
France
   including French Guayana,
   French Polynesia,
   Guadeloupe, Martinique,
   New Caledonia,
   Réunion, St Pierre and
   Miquelon

Greece
Guatemala

Honduras
Hungary

Iceland
Ireland
Israel
Italy
Ivory Coast

Jamaica
Japan

Kenya
Korea (Republic of Korea)

Luxembourg

Malawi
Malaysia
Malta
Mexico
Monaco

Nepal
Netherlands
   including The Dutch Antilles
New Zealand
   including the Cook Islands, Niue,
   Tokelau
Niger
Norway

Panama
Paraguay
Peru
Portugal
   including Macau

San Marino
Singapore
Slovakian Republic
Spain
   including the Spanish
   territories of State in
   North Africa (with Ceuta,
   Melilla)
Sweden
Switzerland and Liechtenstein

Togo

United States of America
   including the American
   Virgin Islands,
   American Samoa, Guam,
   Puerto Rica
Uruquay

Venezuela

Yugoslavia

Annex II   Foreigners Act Directive

A5.2 1. For holders of passports from:

Chad
El Salvador
Ghana
Korea (Republic of Korea)
Pakistan
Philippines
Senegal
Thailand
Turkey

2. and holders of diplomatic-passports from:

India
Morocco

It is not compulsory to have a visa.

Annex III   Foreigners Act Directive

A5.3 Afghanistan
Angola
Bangladesh
Bulgaria
Ethiopia
(The) Gambia
Ghana
Iran

Iraq
Jordan
Lebanon
Nigeria
Romania
Somalia
Sri Lanka
Syria

Greece

Chapter 6
Greece

1. Permanent immigrants

(i) Employment

(a) Work permits

THE PRINCIPLE

Any citizen of a non-EC country entering Greece with the intention of working **6.1** as an employee must have obtained prior approval with the necessary work permit, in order to enter the country

Such prior approval is granted by the Ministry of Foreign Affairs, which authorises the competent consulate of the area where the foreign citizen resides to provide the latter with a consulate employment visa.

THE EXCEPTIONS

Exceptionally the prior approval of a work permit is not necessary for: **6.2**

(i)   Foreign employees of commercial, industrial or shipping companies that have no branch or subsidiary in Greece, but are established in Greece under a special status only for the purpose of managing their business transactions out of Greece (Law 89/1967 as in force). The foreign employees of such companies are entitled to a two-year work and residence permit which can be extended indefinitely for a two-year period each time, as long as the relevant company operates under the same status.

(ii)   Foreign technicians with special scientific or technical knowledge, who cannot be replaced by Greek employees with an equivalent background and knowledge and are employed in industries or mines for a period of three months maximum, in order to urgently repair machinery or other installations.

(iii)   Foreign athletes who are employed by sports associations or clubs, under the special terms and conditions expressly provided by Greek Law with regard to the maximum number of foreign athletes that such associations are allowed to employ.

(iv)   Foreign press correspondents who are legally accredited in Greece and have obtained the relevant certificate of the Ministry of Presidency.

(v)   Foreign coach drivers who are hired by sports associations or clubs according to the provisions and restrictions expressly provided by Greek Law.

(vi)   One foreign employee per tourist agency, under the condition that the agency does not employ other foreigners, brings an important number of tourists to Greece and contributes to the national economy, as certified by the National Tourism Organisation.

(vii)   Directors of foreign airline companies and their deputies, under the condition that the Civil Aviation Authority consents thereto.

(viii)   Tour leaders, under the condition that the National Tourism Organisation consents thereto.

(ix)   Teaching personnel of foreign schools that are recognised and operating in Greece, under the condition that the Ministry of Education consents thereto.

(x)   Members of artistic groups who enter Greece as part of educational exchanges under the supervision of the Ministry of Culture and the Organisations of Local Administration, under the condition that they apply to the Ministries of Foreign Affairs and of Public Order at least 20 days before the beginning of the performance.

6.3   All foreigners who have entered the country according to the above procedure, *i.e.* both those who need prior approval of a work permit before coming to Greece and those who do not, must appear before the police department of the area where they stay, together with their employer, and file the necessary documents to obtain the work permit, within one month of their arrival.

Foreign press correspondents, as well as members of artistic groups mentioned in (iv) and (x) above, are exempt from the obligation to obtain a work permit.

6.4   Work permits are granted for a specific time period for a specific job, in a specific area, with a specific employer. Work permits are issued only after taking into consideration the possibility of covering the relevant employment position by unemployed people already residing in Greece, namely by Greek citizens, EC citizens, persons of Greek origin or refugees permanently residing in Greece.

(b) Residence permits

6.5   Foreigners who have entered Greece after having obtained prior approval of the necessary work permit, are granted a one-year residence permit, which may be renewed annually for up to five years.

(ii) Business

(a) Work permits

6.6   Any citizen of a non-EC country who wishes to work in Greece either as a professional, or in order to establish in Greece a personal business or a company, must apply to the Greek consulate of his country for the prior approval of a work permit.

The application and supporting documents are sent by the relevant Greek consulate to the Ministry of Labour, together with a report of the commercial attaché in respect of the business credit and the business activities of the applicant.

The relevant prior approval of a work permit is granted by the Ministry of Labour after taking into consideration the kind of business and the amount of foreign currency to be brought into Greece by the applicant.

Within one month from the day they entered the country, foreign **6.7** professionals and businessmen must appear before the police department of the area where they are staying and file the documents necessary to obtain the work permit. Among such documents, foreign professionals and businessmen have to submit a certificate of the Bank of Greece for the amount of foreign currency they have imported into Greece and converted into GRD (Greek drachma). The relevant work permit is granted for one year and may be renewed, as long as the foreigner's professional activities are profitable for the Greek economy.

(b) Residence permits

Foreign businessmen or professionals who have obtained the prior approval of **6.8** a work permit are granted a one-year residence permit, which may be renewed annually for five years.

(iii) Family and marriage

(a)   Work permits

No prior approval for the issue of a work permit is required for foreigners who **6.9** have been married to Greek citizens, under the condition that the couple lives together and their marriage has lasted for at least two years or that they are parents of a child under 18 years old having Greek nationality.

(b)   Residence permits

Family members of a foreigner who has obtained a work and residence permit **6.10** are granted a special residence permit, the duration and conditions of which are the same as those of the residence permit of the said foreigner. Family members are considered to be the husband/wife, the unmarried children under 18 years old and the parents of the foreigner, under the condition that they are living with and have been supported by the said foreigner.

2. Visitors, students and short-term residence

(i) Students

Foreigners entering Greece to undertake studies in local schools are granted a **6.11** one-year residence permit that is renewed annually until they graduate.

For the issue or renewal of students' residence permits their progress, duration of studies for each academic year, the availability of sufficient means for their subsistence, studying expenses and medical care, are taken into consideration. It is also necessary that no important objections related to public order, security and public health exist.

(ii) Visitors

6.12   All foreigners can enter Greece, provided thay have a regular and valid passport or other equivalent document recognised by international treaties and have obtained a valid visa, if required.

    Such foreigners can stay provisionally in the country for up to three months without any further license from the competent authorities being required. If a visa is required, its duration cannot exceed a three-month period.

6.13   However, if the relevant foreiger has entered Greece with the intention of being employed or working as a professional or businessman, he must have obtained prior approval for a work permit.

(ii) Short-term residence

6.14   Foreigners who are older than 18 years and who have entered Greece for tourism or for any other purpose, other than employment or as a student or as a family member of a foreign employee, and who wish to stay in Greece for a short period of time, must appear personally before the competent police authorities of the area where they are staying, at least 15 days before the expiration of their three-month provisional stay permit and apply for an extension.

6.15   Such a provisional stay permit cannot be extended for more than a further three-month period. Before granting a short-term residence permit, the police authorities take into consideration the purpose of further residing in Greece, the existence or not of satisfactory means of living, the validity and term of the applicant's passport or other equivalent documents, if there is any guarantee that the foreigner can re-enter his country of origin, the intention of long-term residence in Greece and other reasons regarding public health and the social or public interest in general.

3. Refugees and political asylum

6.16   Refugees have to apply for their recognition as such and the issue of a residence permit as soon as they arrive at the border, or at the nearest public authority in cases where they have entered the country illegally. No foreigner can be recognised as a refugee unless he comes directly from a country where his life and/or freedom are in danger in the sense provided for by article 1 of the Geneva Convention.

    Exceptionally, it is acceptable for a foreigner residing or staying in Greece to apply for his recognition and protection as a refugee if the danger against his life and/or freedom emerged after he entered the country.

If a foreigner's application to be protected as a refugee has been irrevocably **6.17** rejected, the Minister of Public Order can only exceptionally and for humanitarian reasons allow him to stay in Greece until he is able to leave the country.

4. Permanent residence and nationality

Any foreigner who is at least 18 years old may apply for naturalisation as a **6.18** Greek citizen.

In order to have the right to apply for Greek nationality, the applicant must have stayed in Greece, (a) for at least eight years in total within the last decade before the application is filed, or (b) for at least three years after the relevant application is filed.

Children of a foreigner who acquires Greek nationality automatically **6.19** become Greek citizens, if at the time of their parent's naturalisation they are under 18 years old and unmarried.

Marriage does not have any effect on either obtaining or losing Greek nationality.

5. Sanctions

A foreigner is liable to deportation if: **6.20**
(i)   he has been convicted and given a prison sentence by the Greek court;
(ii)   he violates Greek immigration legislation regarding the obligation of foreigners to obtain work and residence permits;
(iii)   his presence in Greece is considered dangerous for public order or health or for the security of the country;
(iv)   he appears before the Greek authorities with different nationalities.

Foreigners who stay in Greece for more than 30 days after the expiration of **6.21** their residence permit, or their permit of provisional stay, are liable to pay at departure an amount equal to double the fee payable for the issue of a residence permit.

If they have illegally stayed in Greece for more than 30 days, they are liable to a fine of 50,000–200,000 GRD.

Any person who violates the immigration laws is liable to imprisonment of up to six months or to a fine or to both according to the Greek Penal Code.

Ireland

Chapter 7
Ireland

Introduction

The guidelines contained in this chapter concerning the rights of aliens to **7.1** reside, work, and/or establish a business in Ireland should be viewed with full cognisance of Ireland's inherent features.

These features include Ireland's:
(i)   geographical position on the periphery of the European Community;
(ii)   economic climate;
(iii)   historical emigration trends;
(iv)   implementation of aliens legislation; and
(v)   European Community obligations.

Minister for Justice

The Minister for Justice (Minister) has sole responsibility for implementing **7.2** aliens legislation in Ireland. The Minister is given wide discretion concerning all matters of entry, residence and employment of aliens. There is no appeal against any decision and/or condition the Minister may make or impose as he thinks appropriate to the entry, residency and employment of an alien. However, all such decisions are subject to judicial review by the High Court and Supreme Court of Ireland, which is a procedure which deals with the decision-making process as opposed to the decision on/or condition of entry, residency and employment.

The definition of aliens does not include persons born in Great Britain **7.3** and/or Northern Ireland, and accordingly such nationals are treated in the same way as Irish nationals. There exists a common travel area between the two jurisdictions and there is no passport control in respect of persons travelling to and from each country. Nationals of Great Britain and Northern Ireland are therefore not subject to:
(i)   visa requirements;
(ii)   work permits;
(iii)   business permit; or
(iv)   aliens registration.

Legislation

All persons who are not citizens of Ireland are described as "aliens". The **7.4** Aliens Act 1935 and the Alien Orders 1946–91 regulate the position of aliens wishing to enter, reside, work or establish a business in Ireland.

General principles applicable to permanent and temporary immigrants

Visa requirements

7.5 The current legislation, requires certain aliens to obtain from the Department of Justice a valid visa prior to presenting himself at a port of entry. For a complete list see Appendix (A) at the end of this chapter. Unless an alien is a citizen of a state specified in this Appendix a valid Irish visa will be required.

7.6 Any alien to whom the visa requirements apply, who proposes to take up employment or establish himself within the state, must specify his intention in a visa application, which application should be supported by relevant documentation such as an application for a work permit and/or a grant of a work permit. If an alien requiring a visa proposes to establish a business in Ireland, details of the said business venture together with business plan and evidence of available finance should be referred to in the visa application. The alien must specify the purpose of travel to Ireland as a visa will only be valid for that purpose. Should an alien wish to change his immigration status while in Ireland, it is the government's stated policy to request the alien to leave the jurisdiction and reapply for a new visa.

Further certain aliens may be required to obtain a transit visa for the purposes of transitting the state.

Leave to land/enter

7.7 At the port of entry, an immigration officer has extensive powers to refuse leave to land to an alien coming from a place outside the state other than Great Britain and Northern Ireland. The immigration officer can rely, *inter alia*, on the following grounds (this is not an exhaustive list):
(i)   the alien is not in a position to support himself and any accompanying dependants;
(ii)   the alien does not hold a valid work permit although wishing to take up employment in the state;
(iii)   the alien does not hold a valid Irish visa;
(iv)   the alien is not in possession of a valid passport or other document which establishes his nationality and identity;
(v)   the alien intends to travel to Great Britain or Northern Ireland and the immigration officer is satisfied that the alien would not qualify for admission to Great Britain or Northern Ireland.

7.8 An alien arriving into the state from Great Britain or Northern Ireland who is not a national of a country specified in Appendix A hereto must have a valid Irish visa issued for the purpose of the travel.

An alien entering Ireland from Great Britain or Northern Ireland who proposes to engage in employment or establish himself in business is required to report to the registration officer of the district in which he intends to reside within seven days of arrival in the state and produce valid identity documentation establishing his nationality. Further, such an alien must not remain in the state for longer than one month without the written permission of the Minister.

Any other alien entering the country from Great Britain or Northern **7.9**
Ireland who does not propose to engage in employment or establish himself in
business shall not remain in the state for longer than a three-month period
without completing registration and obtaining the written permission of the
Minister to remain.

Registration/permission to remain

Every alien subject to the immigration laws must register his presence in the **7.10**
jurisdiction with the Registration Officer for the district in which he resides
after three months.

On registration an alien will obtain a registration certificate and will be
given permission to remain in the jurisdiction for a limited period, usually one
year, which registration and permission must be renewed on the expiration of
the said period.

The obligation to register with the Registration Authority and/or possession
of valid documentation does not apply to aliens under 16 years of age.

1. Permanent immigrants

(i) Employment

(a) Employees granted work permits

The Department of Labour has the responsibility for issuing work permits to **7.11**
alien nationals and has as its aim preservation of jobs for Irish/EC nationals.

Every alien is obliged to obtain a work permit prior to his arrival in Ireland,
which application is processed by the prospective employer. Work permits will
only be issued where the employer can satisfy the Department of Labour that
there is no Irish/EC national with the appropriate professional or technical
skills required for the particular job. Usually the employer must prove that
attempts were made to recruit from local/EC markets by advertising locally,
nationally and with Sedoc recruiting offices in Europe.

Applications will usually receive a favourable consideration from the **7.12**
Department if it can be shown that the granting of a work permit will create
job opportunities for Irish/EC nationals in the short- or long-term.

An alien engaged in employment in the state, having entered the state with a
valid work permit in respect of that employment and who now wishes to take
up a different employment instead may, depending on the particular
circumstances, be required to leave the country and re-enter having received,
prior to re-entry, a valid work permit in respect of proposed new employment.
A similar provision also applies in the case of an alien who is solely residing in
Ireland and who subsequently wishes to take up employment within the state.
In both cases the Departments of Justice and Labour should be consulted to see
whether such departure and re-entry will in fact be necessary or whether it will
be possible for the alien to continue residing in the state during this transition

period. The current legislation is silent on the issue. However, practice and policy would indicate that an alien wishing to change his immigration status can be required to leave the state.

7.13   When the work permit is issued it relates to a specific employee and a specific job with a specific employer.

The work permit requirement is universal, applying to all aliens no matter how short the duration of stay will be. Performing artists, such as musicians and actors, also require work permits. Such applications are usually automatically granted.

(b) Exceptions on the grounds of Irish ancestry

7.14   Only non-Irish non-EC nationals require work permits. Persons of Irish descent, though not born in Ireland, as defined by the Irish Nationality of Citizenship Acts 1956–86, do not require same.

(c) Trainees

7.15   No distinction is made in the governing legislation and regulations between trainees and those engaged in full gainful employment. All aliens who propose to work in Ireland, however short the duration or purpose, are obliged to apply for work permits.

(d) Permit free employment

7.16   There is no such category.

(e) Sole representatives of overseas firms

7.17   Such persons are also subject to the work permit provisions. However, there are usually cogent arguments for granting such representatives permits on grounds of prospective investment and/or employment for Irish/EC nationals. Further, it is accepted that persons with prior knowledge of a particular skill and knowledge of company policy are necessary and essential when an overseas firm is setting up a branch business in Ireland.

(f) Doctors and dentists

7.18   Within the European Community there is free movement of persons which incorporates the right of establishment and the right to provide and receive a service. The fundamental EC principle is applicable to doctors and dentists. Outside the European Community the standard work/business permit conditions apply to such professions.

(g) Overseas journalists and broadcasters

7.19   There are no privileges pertaining to such persons as the work permit requirement applies to all aliens wishing to take up employment.

(ii) **Business**

(a) Businessmen and businesswomen

All business persons wishing to establish a business in Ireland must obtain a   **7.20**
business permit from the Minister. There are no statutory or regulatory
guidelines published. However, the policy implemented by the government in
the past has clearly been influenced by the UK requirements.

Essentially, such business persons must satisfy certain monetary criteria on
the minimum amount to be invested and proof that while in Ireland they will
be in a position to support themselves and not be a burden on the state. A
business permit application should consist of a business plan, projected figures
and will usually receive favourable consideration if the applicant can satisfy
the Minister as to the real and potential prospect of employment of Irish/EC
nationals.

(iii) **Persons of independent means/investors**

The current legislation does not create a special category of persons of   **7.21**
independent means/investors. Any alien who does not wish to take up
employment and or establish a business but who wishes to stay in Ireland in
excess of three months will be obliged to register and obtain the written
permission of the Minister to remain. The immigration official will satisfy
himself that the person has sufficient means to support himself and, where
appropriate, any necessary dependants. The Minister has a very wide
discretion in all matters of the entry, residence and/or employment of aliens.

(iv) **Family and marriage**

The current legislation and alien orders relate to all aliens. There is no absolute   **7.22**
right for dependants to accompany an alien, although such permission will
normally be granted once an alien can satisfy the Immigration Officer at the
port of entry and the Minister that he is in a position to support each
dependant so that they will not become a burden on the state. Registration
requirements and the requirement to obtain permission to remain in the state
shall equally apply to such dependants.

(a) Marriage

Aliens married to Irish nationals will, subject to fulfilling certain requirements,   **7.23**
be entitled to Irish citizenship after a period of three years. In the intervening
period the provisions relating to registration and obtaining work permits will
apply. Leave to land will generally be granted. However, an Immigration
Officer may refuse entry on the groupds that the purpose of entry to Ireland is
primarily to obtain admission to the United Kingdom and is satisfied that the
alien would not qualify for admission to the United Kingdom if entering from
a place other than Ireland.

(b) Children born in Ireland

7.24   Pursuant to the Irish Nationality and Citizenship Acts 1956–86, every person born in Ireland is an Irish citizen from birth. Notwithstanding the nationality of the parents, who may be obliged to comply with the current immigration regulations, persons born in Ireland are exempt.

(c) Other children

7.25   Children under the age of 16 are not obliged to comply with registration requirements described previously and their admission with alien parents will be automatic.

(d) Adopted children

7.26   Once an adoption order has been made in favour of the parents who are Irish nationals, the child is accorded the same equal rights as those accorded to the parents' natural issue.

(e) Exceptions for UK nationals

7.27   As previously explained, the definition of an "alien" does not include persons born in Great Britain and/or Northern Ireland. Such nationals are treated as though they were Irish.

2. Students, visitors and temporary workers

(i) Visitors

7.28   A visitor although not defined is clearly understood to mean a person who does not intend to remain in the state in excess of three months. Thereafter, the procedure outlined above with regard to registration and applying for permission to remain will apply. The concept is usually associated with tourists and holidaymakers and, unless an immigration officer at point of entry is not satisfied as to the purpose of travel or the appropriate visas have not been obtained, such persons receive little attention by same.

(ii) Business visits

7.29   Persons entering Ireland to transact business or attend conferences are treated liberally by the Immigration Officers. Persons *may* be asked to provide some proof of the purpose of the visit.

(iii) Students

7.30   Aliens wishing to study in the state must provide the Immigration Officer at the port of entry with proof of:
(i)   enrolment on a particular course;

(ii)   payment of fees;

(iii)   financial support for the course period; and

(iv)   valid passport, and/or visa.

The Immigration Officer must be satisfied that the course is full-time, bona fide, and that the proposed student will not become a burden on the state.

(iv) Prospective students

Aliens who wish to change their immigration status from that as a visitor to a student or worker may be required to leave the state and re-apply for a student visa or work permit.   **7.31**

(v) Medical students

(See para 6.30)   **7.32**

(vi) Wives and children of students

(See paras 6.22–6.27)   **7.33**

(vii) Au pairs

There is no official category for au pairs.   **7.34**

(viii) Working holidaymakers

US and Canadian students may obtain temporary holiday work visas on a reciprocal basis as is afforded Irish Nationals by the US and Canadian authorities. The students must prove they are in full-time education and that they propose to return to same after the maximum period of four months.   **7.35**

3. Refugees and political asylum

Set out in Appendix B at the end of this chapter are the Conventions and Protocols to which Ireland is a party. Ireland's position is similar to that pertaining in the United Kingdom in that it is a signatory to the convention and to the protocol relating to the status of refugees. However, neither the 1951 Convention nor the 1967 protocol have been incorporated directly into Irish law.   **7.36**

Due, *inter alia*, to Ireland's geographical position and economic climate, the number of asylum seekers and refugee applications to the Department of Justice is significantly less than any of its European counterparts.

Persons who have a well founded fear of persecution for reasons of race, religion, nationality, membership of a social group or political opinion may   **7.37** apply for refugee status: (a) to an individual immigration officer on arrival at port of entry, (b) if already in the country directly to the Department of Justice or (c) to the Irish Consul abroad.

Whether or not an individual is an asylum seeker is a matter of fact to be decided in the light of all the information and circumstances as may be available in any particular case.

Guide-lines have been produced following negotiations between represent-atives of the United Nations High Commission for Refugees and the Department of Foreign Affairs. These guide-lines are not binding on Ireland and are merely designed to regularise refugee applications.

7.38 It is important to note that there is no UNHCR office in Ireland although there is a UNHCR representative accredited to Ireland. The guide-lines provide that an individual seeking asylum will not be refused entry, and will not be removed from the state until (i) he has been provided with the opportunity of presenting his case fully, (ii) his application has been properly examined and (iii) a decision reached on it.

It is not unusual for the Department to seek the view of the UNHCR in difficult cases. Once an applicant has been recognised as a refugee a travel document certifying his status will be issued. On obtaining such status there is no automatic right for the refugee to bring his family to Ireland.

Where a refugee fails to establish his status pursuant to the 1951 convention he may be permitted to remain in the state on "humanitarian grounds".

4. Permanent residence and nationality

7.39 The Minister has power to naturalise aliens of whatever category and immigration status provided, *inter alia*, certain legal residence requirements are fulfilled. Any applicant for naturalisation must have a total of five years' legal residence within the state out of the previous eight with the last year being continuous residence.

Further the Minister may in his absolute discretion grant an application for naturalisation notwithstanding legal residence requirements have not been fulfilled where, *inter alia*, the applicant is of Irish association or Irish descent.

5. Discretion

7.40 The Minister has absolute discretion in all immigration matters from which there is *no* appeal.

6. Sanctions

7.41 The Minister may, whenever he thinks proper, by order make provision for the exclusion and/or deportation of an alien from the state.

7. **Detention**

An alien, in respect of whom a Deportation Order is made or a recommenda-   **7.42**
tion is made by a court with a view to the making of a Deportation Order, may
be detained in such a manner as may be directed by the Minister.

Any person acting in contravention of the Aliens Orders 1946–91 may be
taken into custody without warrant by an Immigration Officer or by any
member of the *Gardai Siochana* (national police force).

Appendix A – Visa exemptions

Nationals of the following countries do not require a visa for Ireland.

Andorra	Nauru
Argentina	Netherlands
Australia	New Zealand
Austria	Nicaragua
	Norway
Bahamas	
Barbados	Panama
Belgium	Paraguay
Botswana	Portugal
Brazil	
	San Marino
Canada	Sierra Leone
Chile	Singapore
Costa Rica	Slovak Republic
Cyprus	South Africa
Czech Republic	Spain
	Swaziland
Denmark	Sweden
	Switzerland
Ecuador	
El Salvador	Tanzania
	Trinidad and Tobago
Fiji	
Finland	Uganda
France	United Kingdom and Colonies*
	United Republic of Tonga
Gambia	United States of America
Germany	Uruguay
Greece	
Grenada	Vatican City
Guatemala	Venezuela
Guyana	
	Western Samoa
Honduras	
Hungary	Zambia
	Zimbabwe
Iceland	
Israel	Transit visas are required for:
Italy	Bulgaria, Iran, Moldavia, Sri Lanka
Jamaica	
Japan	

Kenya
Korea (South)

Lesotho
Liechtenstein
Luxembourg

Malawi
Malaysia
Malta
Mauritius
Mexico
Monoco

---

* British Dependent Territories (Colonies): Anguila, Bermuda, British Antarctic Territory (South Georgia, South Sandwich Islands), British Indian Ocean Territory (Chagos Archipelago, Peros Banos Diego Garcia, Danger Island), Cayman Islands, Falkland Islands and dependencies, Gibraltar, Hong Kong (however, a person in possession of a Hong Kong Certificate of Identity requires an entry visa for the State), Montserrat, Pitcairn (Henderson, Ducie and Oneno Islands), St Helena and dependencies (Ascension Island, Tristan Da Cunha), the Sovereign based areas of Akrotiri and Dhekelia, Turks and Caicos Islands, British Virgin Islands.

Appendix B – Refugee status

A7.2 1. Convention Relating to the Status of
Refugees
Geneva 28 July 1951
Irish Instrument of Accession deposited on 29 November 1956

2. Convention Relating to the Status of
Stateless Persons
New York 20 September 1954
Irish Instrument of Accession deposited on 19 December 1962

3. The European Agreement on the
Abolition of Visas for Refugees
Strasbourg 20 April 1959
Entering into force in Ireland 30
November 1959

4. Protocol Relating to the Status of
Refugees
New York 21 January 1969
This extends a concept of refugees to
events occurring outside Europe.

Italy

Chapter 8
Italy

1. Permanent immigrants

(i) Employment

(a) Employees granted work permits

Work Permits are issued by the Head of Police (*Questore*). **8.1**

A specific visa is required and a certificate from the Labour Office must be obtained. Extensions can be obtained by proving that the same circumstances exist as at the time of the original application. Procedures are simplified for specific categories of employment which are in much demand in Italy, for example nurses.

(b) *"Oriundi"*

Foreign nationals who have Italian ancestors and former nationals are known **8.2** as *Oriundi*. It is possible to reclaim citizenship on grounds of *jus sanguinus* for those of Italian descent and it is not too complicated to obtain a work permit for former nationals having lost Italian citizenship within less than five years. After two years of residence in Italy, former nationals can automatically regain their citizenship.

(c) Employees of a branch company in Italy

It is necessary to prove that the company pays the employee in the foreign **8.3** country and the length of the employment in Italy must be stipulated either for employment or self-employment. A visa from an Italian Embassy abroad is mandatory.

(d) Artists

Again, a visa from an Italian Embassy abroad is mandatory specifically for the **8.4** artist. The artist must then register with the Employment Office (Showbusiness Department).

(ii) Religious reasons

A specific visa from an Italian Embassy abroad is mandatory. The applicant **8.5** must produce a statement from the congregation to which he/she has been invited.

(iii) Business

8.6   For the self-employed it is mandatory to have a visa before entering Italy. It is necessary to obtain a licence from the local Chamber of Commerce and/or to be accepted by the National Professional Category Councils in order to work as a self-employed professional. Procedures in order to obtain licences from the Chamber of Commerce or authorisation by National Professional Category Councils are very detailed and require the attendance of the applicant for a period of training and/or a course organised by the Chamber of Commerce. A specific College Diploma is required. In some cases, a company might act as a sponsor.

(iv) Family

8.7   A visa for family reasons is necessary. A family residence permit will not be granted on a tourist's visa. It is necessary to satisfy the Italian Authorities, by presenting a marriage certificate or proof of married status obtained from the Consulate. After three years of effective legal residence, if married to an Italian, a residence permit will be granted for family reasons for an unlimited period.

(v) Co-habitation

8.8   On the basis of co-habitation, a residence permit will not normally be granted. Only in the most exceptional circumstances can discretion be exercised in favour of a couple seeking a residence permit on co-habitation grounds. Even if a residence permit was granted, this would not permit the couple (or either of them) to apply for a work permit.

(vi) Children and minors

8.9   Parental status must be proven by a passport or birth certificate from the competent Consulate in order to register children on the residence permits of parents. A specific visa must be obtained from the Italian Embassy before entry into Italy.

2. Visitors, students and temporary workers

8.10   For some specific countries a visa is required in order to obtain a permit. A three months' residence period is normally granted. Frontier Police must place a dated entry stamp on the passport of non-EC nationals who enter the country. The data of non-EC nationals are to be collected as well by the Frontier Police and sent to the database of the Ministry of the Interior. Refusal of entry must be given in writing. This decision can be appealed to the Regional Administrative Tribunal.

As for students, a specific visa is necessary. Evidence of university enrolment, **8.11** insurance and consular statement for admission to university are required. If a student is attending school rather than university, the consular statement is not required.

If medical treatment in Italy is being sought, a statement about the need for therapy in Italy must be produced to the Italian Embassy.

3. **Refugees and political asylum**

The recognition of the status of refugees can be acquired by persons coming **8.12** from any part of the world. Italy has renounced the clause of geographical limits contained in the Geneva Convention of 1951. Foreign nationals are not allowed to apply for the status of refugee if they were granted refugee status by another country or if they have committed serious crimes against humanity or been convicted in Italy of crimes relating to drug trafficking or terrorism.

Foreign nationals can appeal to the Regional Administrative Tribunal.

4. **General**

Article 2 of Law No. 39/90 says that foreign non-EC nationals are allowed to **8.13** enter Italy for reasons of tourism, study, employment, self-employment, medical treatment, religious purposes and family reasons.

In order to enter Italy, foreign nationals should present a valid passport or **8.14** document recognised by the Italian authorities together with a visa required according to a list of countries provided by the Minister of Foreign Affairs, approved by the Minister of the Interior. The list of countries from which visas are required is revised every year within the context of bi-lateral and multi-lateral agreements. The visa issued by the competent diplomatic or consulate authorities will specify the reason for entry, length of stay and the number of entries into Italian territory (when applicable). Foreign nationals who do not fulfil this requirement will not be accepted by the Frontier Police. The Frontier Police must also refuse those visa holders who have previously been expelled, have been identified as a danger to the security of the state or who belong to criminal or drug trafficking or terrorist organisations.

Foreign nationals who are without any visible means of support are to be **8.15** refused as well, unless they can provide proof of support including documents of property in Italy or regular income from employment. A religious body, an association or a private person can "sponsor" and guarantee financial support.

or to the need to give financial support and can justify the fact that the
widow of a [illegible] was...

to introduce adequate measures such as [illegible] schemes and other
means to enable students to attend [illegible] school or job-seekers... the
child is attending school rather than knowing the conditions that gave rise
to...

It must importantly be held in [illegible] more by a family in which the power
that..., the child is supported or deprived of material...

3. Refugees and political asylum

The present position of persons of foreign origin [illegible] in [illegible] of the person asking, during
[illegible] and persons in the sense. This is has appeared the [illegible] as a [illegible] political
[illegible] in accordance to the Geneva Convention of 1951, is not [illegible] to be...
able [illegible] to [illegible] the [illegible] of [illegible] of [illegible]...
[illegible]...
[illegible] for [illegible] of [illegible]...
[illegible] are [illegible] may not to the [illegible]...

1. General

Before the Law No. [illegible] only [illegible] [illegible] [illegible] [illegible] [illegible]...
under Italian law [illegible]...
and their [illegible] religion, surroundings and family members.

[illegible] to [illegible] foreign nationals should [illegible] in a [illegible]...
foreigner were [illegible] by the Italian authorities with a [illegible] a [illegible] of
[illegible] on the [illegible]...
expressed by the Ministry or plain [illegible]. The [illegible] and [illegible]...
[illegible] turned in several cases. [illegible]...
[illegible] authorities.... The [illegible] is [illegible]...
[illegible] author has [illegible]. In the case of the [illegible]...
[illegible] of claim is a [illegible]...
who do not fulfil the [illegible]...
The [illegible] Police have [illegible]...
[illegible] [illegible] have been [illegible]...
[illegible]...

A foreign national is among [illegible]...
[illegible] will [illegible]...
[illegible]...
[illegible]...

Luxembourg

Chapter 9
Luxembourg*

Introduction

This chapter provides a synopsis of the situation in the Grand-Duchy of **9.1** Luxembourg with respect to foreign immigration, including but not limited to, its history, regulatory policies and trends.

By way of introduction, the Grand-Duchy of Luxembourg is a country which can boast the most significant proportion of foreigners on its territory compared to the rest of Europe (and perhaps the world).

To this impressive number of foreigners residing in Luxembourg, there must be added the numerous cross-frontier workers who transit Luxembourg's borders each day to exercise their profession in the Grand-Duchy, such that 40–50% of the working population is composed of foreigners.

Luxemburgers are, as a consequence, in daily contact with a number of **9.2** foreigners which has no equivalent in any other European state, a fact that easily explains the benevolent attitude which the government and population exhibits towards the foreign population. Luxemburgers are conscious that, without this foreign strength, their entire economy would suffer. As a result, the Grand-Duchy of Luxembourg's legislation concerning foreigners is not only quite liberal, but also less burdensome than that of other countries.

1. Citizenship and nationality

Matters of citizenship and nationality are governed by the law dated 22 **9.3** February 1968 which was modified in 1975, 1977 and 1986 (*Loi sur la nationalité luxembourgeoise* and hereinafter referred to as the "Nationality law").

By virtue of article 1 of this law, the following persons are considered to be **9.4** natives of Luxembourg:

(i)   A child who is born in a foreign country from a progenitor of Luxumburgish nationality, if the descent of the child is established before the age of 18 years, and if the progenitor is a Luxemburger at the moment of the establishment of the descent.

If the judgment establishing the descent is only pronounced after the death of the father or the mother, the child will be a native of Luxembourg, if the progenitor had Luxemburgish nationality at death.

---

* Previously published in part by Martinus Nijhoff Publishers, a member of the Kluwer Academic Publishers Group, in 1993.

(ii)　A child who is born in the Grand-Duchy of Luxembourg and whose parents are unknown.

A child who is found on the Luxembourg territory is presumed to be born in the Grand-Duchy of Luxembourg, until the contrary is proven.

(iii)　A child who was born in Luxembourg and who has no other nationality.

9.5　According to article 2 of the Nationality Law, the following persons will acquire Luxembourg nationality:

(i)　A child who was adopted by a Luxemburger by way of a plenary adoption (*adoption plénière*).

(ii)　A child who has not yet attained the age of 18 years and who has been adopted by a Luxemburger by way of a simple adoption (*adoption simple*), if this child is either stateless or has lost his original nationality as a result of this adoption.

(iii)　A child who has not yet attained the age of 18 and whose progenitor or adopter voluntarily acquires or receives Luxembourg nationality.

(i) Naturalisation

9.6　The process of naturalisation must be introduced by a written request addressed to the Minister of Justice, who then deliberates with the city council of the foreigner's residence (art 9 ad 10, Nationality Law).

9.7　After this, the request will be submitted to the parliament which will have to grant the naturalisation by law (*ibid*, at art 13). The foreigner must then accept this naturalisation by a declaration to the civil status officer (*ibid*, art 15). The naturalisation will be effective four days after the publication of the notice indicating the date of its acceptance in the official gazette (*Mémorial*), (*ibid*, art 18). Different conditions must, however, be fulfilled by the person in order to benefit from the naturalisation process foreseen by article 6 of the Nationality Law. Specifically, the subject must:

(i)　have reached the age of 18;

(ii)　have resided in the Grand-Duchy of Luxembourg for at least ten years, the last five years of which must have been without interruption.

9.8　The obligatory residence period of ten years can be reduced to five years in the following situations:

- the applicant is stateless;
- the applicant was born on Luxembourg territory;
- the applicant is a widow of a Luxemburger of origin from whom he has one or several children alive and of which at least one is established in Luxembourg;
- the applicant is a divorced spouse and a Luxemburger of origin and has one or several children alive whose custody was attributed to him and at least one of whom is residing in Luxembourg;
- the applicant is without nationality unless the loss of his anterior nationality resulted from his express demand or from the demand of his legal representative;

– the applicant is recognised as a refugee by virtue of the Convention on Refugees signed at Geneva on 28 July 1951.

The naturalisation can also be accorded without satisfying the condition of **9.9** residence, if the applicant has rendered special services to the state of Luxembourg.

The law of 11 December 1986 modifying the Nationality Law has introduced a particular disposition in case of marriage. An applicant married to a person who fulfills the above-mentioned conditions and who also requests authorisation must have his residence on the territory of Luxembourg for three years, and must live in community with his spouse. The condition of age does not have to be fulfilled (art 8, Nationality Law).

(ii) Option

The process of option (choice) is introduced by a declaration of option to the **9.10** Minister of Justice who must grant his approval after deliberation with the borough council of the foreigner's residence (art 23, National Law). The declaration of option enters into effect four days after its publication in the official gazette (*ibid*, art 24).

The possibility of a declaration of option only exists in the following **9.11** situations listed in article 19 of the Nationality Law:
(i)   a child born in Luxembourg from a foreign progenitor;
(ii)   a child born in a foreign country from a progenitor having Luxembourg nationality;
(iii)   a foreigner whose spouse either is a Luxemburger, or who acquires or receives the Luxemburgish nationality;
(iv)   a child born in a foreign country from a foreign progenitor who has accomplished his entire obligatory scholarship in the Grand-Duchy of Luxembourg;
(v)   a child having been adopted by way of a simple adoption (*adoption simple*) by a Luxemburger and who has not lost his original nationality at the moment of this adoption;
(vi)   a foreigner having reached the age of 18 and whose progenitor acquires or receives the Luxembourg nationality.

By virtue of article 20 of the Nationality Law a person who finds himself in **9.12** one of the situations (i), (ii), (iv), (v), must have been resident in Luxembourg for an uninterrupted period of five years, as well as during the last year prior to depositing his declaration of option. This declaration must be made between the ages of 18 and 25 years.

The admission of the option in case of situation (iii) above depends upon the following double condition: the subject must have been resident in the Grand-Duchy of Luxembourg for at least three years, and he must live in community with his spouse (*ibid*, art 21).

Moreover, the declaration of option can be rejected in different cases listed **9.13** in article 22 of the Nationality Law, as modified by a law dated 26 June 1975. For example, if the subject does not prove, by way of certificates delivered by the competent authorities, that he has lost his original nationality or that he will automatically lose it by acquiring another nationality (in conformity with the convention on the reduction of the cases of plurality of nationalities dated 6 May 1963 which came into force on 1 January 1991). Furthermore, the option is refused if the person cannot justify a sufficient "assimilation".

Particular attention must be paid to the dispositions concerning married women. In fact, the Grand-Duchy of Luxembourg has signed and ratified the convention on the nationality of married women (2 February 1957) which came into force on 1 January 1991 (hereinafter referred to as the "Married Woman Convention").

9.14 This convention provides that neither the concluding nor the dissolution of a marriage between a Luxemburger and a foreigner, nor the change of nationality by the husband during the marriage, can have any effect on the nationality of the wife (art 1 of the Married Woman Convention).

Furthermore, this convention provides that all the signatory states agree that neither the voluntary acquisition of the nationality of a foreign state by one of its nationals, nor the renunciation of nationality by one of its nationals, will prevent the wife of the national from keeping her nationality (*ibid*, art 2).

Finally, the convention provides that signatory states must accord the right to a foreign woman married to a national to acquire the nationality of her husband through a simplified naturalisation procedure, a disposition effective in the Grand-Duchy of Luxembourg by virtue of the law of 11 December 1986 (*ibid*, art 3).

2. Entry and temporary visit or sojourn of foreigners

9.15 This matter is governed by the Law of 28 March 1972 concerning:
(i)   entry and sojourn of foreigners;
(ii)   medical control of foreigners;
(iii)   employment of foreign workers.
(hereinafter entitled "Entry and Sojourn Law").

9.16 The Grand-Ducal regulation of the same date concerning the formalities to be fulfilled by foreigners visiting Luxembourg (hereinafter entitled the "Formality Regulation") also impacts upon the matter.

(i) Dispositions regarding an unemployed national of a Non-EC Member State

(a) General dispositions

9.17 By virtue of article 2 of the Entry and Sojourn Law, entry and sojourn in the Grand-Duchy of Luxembourg can be refused to a foreigner in the following cases:
–   if he has neither identification papers nor visa, if such is required;
–   if he could endanger public security, order or health;
–   if he does not have sufficient means to support his travel and sojourn costs.

THE SHORT SOJOURN

A foreigner who does not wish to remain for more than three months in the Grand-Duchy of Luxembourg, must make a declaration to this effect within eight days of his arrival to the local authority of the place where he intends to reside (art 1 of the Formalities Regulation). **9.18**

THE SOJOURN

A foreigner who has attained the age of 15 years, and who wishes to remain in the Grand-Duchy of Luxembourg for more than three months, must also make a declaration to this effect to the local authorities of the place where he wishes to stay, and forthermore, must deposit a request for a foreigner's identity card (*carte d'identité d'étranger*) (*ibid*, art 4). **9.19**

Furthermore, a foreigner who intends to reside in Luxembourg for more than three months must submit himself to a medical examination in order to discover and prevent contagious diseases and drug addiction (art 21 of the Entry and Sojourn Law and art 9 of the Formality Regulation). This medical examination includes:
(i)   an X-ray examination of the lungs; and
(ii)   a medical certificate drawn up by a doctor.

In the event that the foreigner refuses this examination, an authorisation to establish himself on Luxembourg territory can be refused (art 5 of the Entry and Sojourn Law). **9.20**

The foreigner identity card can also be withdrawn (and its renewal refused) if the foreigner stops fulfilling all of the conditions required for its issue, or if he does not respect his duties.

Finally, the foreigner who intends to reside for more than three months has to pay a tax of LUF 1,000.

The above-mentioned decision granting or refusing the delivery of the foreigner identity card is taken by the Minister of Justice, and can be subjected to a juridical remedy before the administrative court (*Conseil d'Etat*). **9.21**

The refusal of authorisation to "sojourn" or of authorisation of establishment, or refusal to issue the foreigner identity card, as well as the withdrawing or the refusal to renew the identity card has, as a direct consequence, the expulsion of the foreigner from the territory of Luxembourg (*ibid*, art 7).

(b) Particular dispositions

EC NATIONALS

Article 1 of the Special Regulation applies to: **9.22**
(i)   EC nationals who intend to come to Luxembourg in order to take up a wage earning position;
(ii)   EC nationals exercising a job which is not wage earning;
(iii)   those EC nationals who, *inter alia*, do not intend to live in the Grand-Duchy of Luxembourg, but who offer, as independent workers, services defined by Article 60 of the Treaty of Rome;

(iv)   those who possess the right to stay in Luxembourg by virtue of EC
        Regulations and Directives;

(v)   the spouses of EC nationals and their descendants of less than 21 years
        or dependants without consideration of nationality;

(vi)   the descendants, ascendants and other members of the family who are
        either dependent upon the persons mentioned in numbers (i)–(iv) or to
        their spouse;

(vii)   EC nationals who have a wage earning job in Luxembourg but who
        have their main residence in a foreign country, under the condition that
        they return to their principal country every day or at least once a week
        (modified by regulation dated 1 October 1981).

9.23   The following dispositions are applicable to the seven above-mentioned
groups:

In order to enter and sojourn in the Grand-Duchy of Luxembourg, these
persons must present their national identity card or a valid passport (or one
which has expired not longer than five years prior) or any other piece of
identification recognised for crossing the border (art 2 of the Special Foreigner
Regulation).

The persons in situations (ii), (iii) and (iv) above, as well as their family
members, must also obtain a permit of residence for nationals of an EC
Member State (Grand-Ducal Regulation of 1 October 1981, modifying art 3
of the Special Foreigner Regulation).

9.24   The residence permit loses its validity if the owner resides outside the
Grand-Duchy of Luxembourg for more than six months, unless this absence is
due to a military obligation in the foreign country (*ibid*, art 3 in fine).

A person who enters the Grand-Duchy of Luxembourg in order to work for
less than three months, does not need a permit of residence but is sufficiently
"covered" by the document permitting his entry at the border. However, such
persons must signal their presence within eight days of their arrival to the local
authorities of the place of their residence (*ibid*, art 7).

PUPILS AND STUDENTS

9.25   There is no particular legislation concerning the admission of foreign pupils
and students to the Grand-Duchy of Luxembourg.

TOURISTS

9.26   In addition to the obligation to carry identity papers or travel documents, the
Law dated 16 August 1975 introduced a control over travellers who are
staying in lodging establishments, hereinafter called the "Lodging Establishments Law".

Whosoever may lodge a person in a hotel, a house, a hostel, a boarding
house, an apartment, an equipped room, a campsite, or a youth hostel, must
fill in a card for every person which indicates both information relative to the
establishment (the name and address of the lodging establishment, the number
of the room, the number of the lodging card), and information about the

traveller (name, christian name, place and date of birth, address of habitual residence, nationality, date of arrival, probable duration of their sojourn, persons accompanying the traveller (wife and children, if younger than 15 years), and the signature of the traveller (*ibid*, art 1 in fine).

This card must be filled in on the date of arrival of the traveller. The landlord **9.27** is obliged to verify the information provided by the traveller relative to his identity with reference to the identity papers (*ibid*, art 1 in fine). The traveller must present his identity papers (*ibid*, art 2). The original of the lodging card must be conserved by the hotel keeper for a period of five years (*ibid*, art 3).

One day after the arrival of the traveller, the second copy of the lodging card **9.28** must be sent by the hotel keeper in the city of Luxembourg to the public security service, and in other localities of the Grand-Duchy of Luxembourg to the local public police squad. (Grand-Ducal Regulation of 1 October 1975 concerning the models of card to be held by hotel keepers, art 6). The first copy will be sent in the first five days of the month following the arrival of the traveller to the central service of statistical and economic studies (*ibid*, art 7).

Non-compliance with these dispositions is punishable by an imprisonment **9.29** of between one and seven days and/or a fine of 501–2,500 LUF. (art 6 of the Lodging Establishments Law 16 August 1975).

By a Law dated 7 March 1979, the Grand-Duchy of Luxembourg has also ratified a convention on the responsibility of the hotel keeper concerning the objects brought in by the traveller (Convention dated 17 December 1962). This convention between the Federal Republic of Germany, Belgium, Cyprus, France, Ireland, Italy, Luxembourg, Malta, and the United Kingdom entered into force 1 January 1991.

(ii) **Employment of foreigners**

The Law of 28 March 1972 concerning the entry and sojourn of foreigners and **9.30** their medical control, as well as the employment of foreign workers (hereinafter called "Entry and Sojourn Law") along with the Grand-Ducal Regulation determining the measures applicable to the employment of the foreign workers on the territory of the Grand-Duchy of Luxembourg, (12 May 1972; hereinafter called "Employment Regulation") govern the employment of foreigners.

(a) General conditions

In order to be employed in the territory of Luxembourg, the foreigner must **9.31** obtain a work permit (*ibid*, art 26). This obligation is, however, lifted for workers coming from one of the EC Member States (*ibid*, art 28).

Different kinds of work permits are issued by the Minister of Labour or his deputy on the advice of the National Service of Labour, which takes into consideration the situation, the evolution and the organisation of the employment market (art 2 of the Employment Regulation).

(i)   Permit A is issued for a period of one year, and valid for one specific profession and only one particular employer.

    (ii)   Permit B is issued for a period of four years, and valid for one specific profession, but any employer.

    (iii)   Permit C is issued for an undetermined period, and valid for any profession and any employer.

    (iv)   Permit D is issued to apprentices and trainees, and valid for the duration of the apprenticeship or the training period.

9.32   The validity of permit A can be extended to one or several other employers, if its holder does execute, in the same profession, partial work for different employers.   By virtue of article 3 of the Employment Regulation, permit C can be accorded to the following persons:

–   workers who can prove that they have either had a residence or an uninterrupted employment for at least five years in the Grand-Duchy of Luxembourg; and

–   workers born in the Grand-Duchy of Luxembourg who have had their residence in the Grand-Duchy of Luxembourg during an uninterrupted period of at least two years prior to their request for a work permit.

9.33   Permit B can be accorded to workers who have either had their residence or a job in the Grand-Duchy of Luxembourg for an uninterrupted period of at least one year.

    Workers who cross the border regularly in order to obtain work (*travailleurs frontaliers*) can obtain a work permit B or C if they have worked on Luxembourg territory for an uninterrupted period of one or five years respectively.

    Finally, permit A can be delivered to all of the other workers who do not fulfill the conditions required for permit B, C or D.

9.34   The work permit loses its validity if its holder is absent from the territory of the Grand-Duchy of Luxembourg for more than six months without interruption. However, this is not the case if the holder of the permit has, in spite of the absence, not interrupted his working relationship with his employer established on the Luxembourg territory.

    In order to employ a foreign worker, the employer must check whether the foreigner is in possession of a valid work permit, and make a declaration to the National Service of Labour (*Office National du Travail*) (*ibid*, art 4). This declaration must be presented in two originals, countersigned by the worker, and shall be considered as a request for obtaining or renewal of a work permit, if it relates to a worker who is not yet in possession of a work permit, or whose work permit has come to the end of its term, or whose work permit is only valid for a specific employer and profession (*ibid*, art 4, para 2). This formality must be accomplished before the worker's entry into employment.

9.35   If an employer desires to recruit a foreign worker who is already in possession of a work permit authorising a change of employer or authorising the worker to be employed by several employers, he must make a preliminary declaration to the National Service of Labour (*ibid*, art 5).

    Article 6 provides that in order to obtain a work permit, the interested party must present an identification paper to the National Service of Labour, which is authorised to verify the worker's professional aptitude. The worker can prove his aptitude by presenting professional certificates or any other documents. If the National Service of Labour decides that the documents presented are insufficient, it can require the worker to take examinations in order to verify his professional aptitude.

The receipt of a work permit can also be subordinated to the conclusion of a **9.36** labour contract between the employer and the worker.

However, some persons are exempt from this obligation of acquiring a work permit. These persons are listed in article 7 of the Employment Regulation. For example, this is the case for:
— the administrative and technical staff of embassies and consulates, at the head of which stands a career agent;
— the domestic staff in the service of a diplomatic agent who is accredited in Luxembourg;
— persons occupied in tasks which overstep national limits or persons who benefit from an international charter;
— the whole staff of fair attractions, circuses, theatres and other travelling establishments, under the condition that they do not stay for longer than one month in the territory of Luxembourg.

For foreign workers temporarily employed on Luxembourg territory within **9.37** their occupation for a Luxembourg or a foreign firm, the Minister of Labour or his deputy can, upon the advice of the National Service of Labour, deliver a collective work permit (*ibid*, art 9). The collective work permit is valid for a period for six months, and only for those jobs and persons specified in the request for its obtention. However, a job accomplished by virtue of a collective work permit does not enable the worker to receive an individual work permit.

Work permits are not automatically issued, but their acquisition can be **9.38** refused for reasons inherent in the situation, as well as the evolution or organisation of the employment market (art 10 of the Employment Regulation). The work permit can be withdrawn in the following situations, listed in article 10:
— if the foreigner has used dishonest practices in order to procure his work permit;
— if he has given false information to the authorities in order to obtain the work permit;
— if he has been working in a profession which is different from the one he is allowed to execute, according to his work permit;
— if his permit of sojourn on the Luxembourg territory has been withdrawn.

Finally, the Employment Regulation also includes criminal penalties (art **9.39** 12). According to the regulation, the following persons will be condemned to a fine of 2,501–50,000 LUF and/or an imprisonment of between 8 days and one month:
(i)   the employer who employs a foreign worker who is not in possession of a work permit although he is obliged to obtain a work permit;
(ii)   the foreigner who executes a job either in violation of the Grand-Ducal Regulation of 12 May 1972, or beyond the limits and conditions of the work permit;

111

(iii)   the foreigner who has intentionally produced falsified or inexact documents in order to obtain a work permit.

9.40   The following persons can be condemned to a fine of 250–2,500 LUF and/or an imprisonment of between one and seven days:

(i)   the employer who has employed a foreigner for a job which is different from the one specified in the latter's work permit;

(ii)   the employer who has employed a foreigner without making the compulsory declaration to the National Service of Labour;

(iii)   any person who tries to impede or retard the control measures undertaken for the execution of the legal dispositions on the employment of foreigners.

(b) Nationals from the Netherlands or Belgium

9.41   As the Grand-Duchy of Luxembourg is a member of the economic union "BENELUX" with the Netherlands and Belgium, some particular dispositions have been introduced into national legislation.

The estabiishment authorisation is accorded to Belgian and Dutch nationals, under the condition that they justify legitimate means of subsistence, and can only be refused in different situations that are exclusively enumerated.

Dutch and Belgian nationals who possess a residence permit for nationals of an EC Member State can only be expelled if they endanger the public order or security.

If they have had their habitual residence in the Grand-Duchy of Luxembourg for more than three years, they cannot be expelled, unless they constitute a danger to either the public national security or the community, as evidenced by being found guilty of a crime or a particularly serious offence.

(c) Refugees and stateless persons

9.42   Refugees and stateless persons who have received a foreigner identity card can only be expelled for reasons of public order or security. Luxembourg has also introduced the different European Directives and Regulations into its legislation.

(d) Dispositions concerning Spanish and Portuguese nationals

9.43   In principle, the dispositions of the Grand-Ducal Regulation of 12 May 1972 determine the measures concerning the employment of foreign workers on Luxembourg territory and the Grand-Ducal Regulation of the same date concerns the medical control of foreigners. However, a Grand-Ducal Regulation of 24 December 1985 specifically concerns the situation of Spanish and Portuguese nationals who are employed in the territory of Luxembourg. This regulation indicates that it only concerns the period as from 1 January 1986 to 31 December 1995.

In spite of this Grand-Ducal resolution, Luxembourg will probably "open" its borders for Spanish and Portuguese workers on 1 January 1993 (see *d'Letzebuerger Land* dated 13 March 1992, p. 3 by Jean-Paul Hoffman).

9.44   By derogation from the regulation of 12 May 1972, Spanish and Portuguese workers must receive a work permit E (for the Spanish workers) or P (for the

Portuguese workers) in order to be allowed to work in the Grand-Duchy of Luxembourg. These work permits E and P are valid for any profession and are not limited in time. However, work permits E and P, which are issued to seasonal workers who have concluded a labour contract for a period of less than 12 months, have their validity limited to the duration of the working relationship.

Spanish and Portuguese nationals who have regularly exercised as of 31 **9.45** December 1985 a wage earning job in Luxembourg and by virtue of a work permit issued in compliance with the above-mentioned Grand-Ducal Regulation, have the right, as of 1 January 1986, to choose without restraint a job on the territory of Luxembourg. To that effect, the Minister of Labour has had to deliver a special title before 1 July 1986 (*ibid.*, art 2).

In addition to the Spanish or Portuguese worker himself, who has exercised **9.46** a regular job in Luxembourg, his spouse and children under 21 years in his charge have free choice of a job and free access to employment under the condition that they have regularly resided with the worker on Luxembourg territory before 13 June 1985 (*ibid*, art 3–1). The spouses and children who have resided regularly in Luxembourg only after 12 June 1985, were subject to the obligation to obtain a work permit until 31 December 1990, and could get a work permit E or P after a minimum residence period of three years (*ibid*, art 3–2). This period has, however, been reduced to 18 months as of 1 January 1989 (*ibid*, art 3–2 in fine).

(e) Au pairs

Luxembourg has ratified the European agreement on the "*placement au pair*" **9.47** (hereinafter referred to as the "Au Pair Agreement"), a convention that came into force on 1 January 1991, between Denmark, France, Spain, Italy, Luxembourg and Norway.

The initial duration of the *placement au pair* may not exceed one year, but can be renewed to permit a sojourn of a maximum two years (art 3 of the Au Pair Agreement). A person who can be placed as an au pair must generally be at least 17 and at most 30 years old, but in exceptional cases, the competent authorities of the state of sojourn can accord a derogation for a superior age limit (*ibid*, art 4). The persons intending to be placed as au pairs must produce a medical certificate established less than three months before their placement, and must indicate their general state of health (*ibid*, art 5). The two parties must conclude a written agreement determining under what conditions the person will share family life, and this should be accomplished preferably before the person has left his country of origin, and at the latest during the first week of his arrival (*ibid*, art 6–1).

The rights of the au pair are determined by article 8 of the Au Pair **9.48** Agreement. The person placed as au pair will be nourished and lodged by the host family, and should, if possible, be able to have use of an individual room. The family must accord to the au pair sufficient time to pursue his linguistic studies and to improve himself on both a cultural and professional level. The au pair has the right to one free day a week, which must be a Sunday, at least once per month. He must also be granted the right to practise his religion. Finally, the au pair will receive pocket money, the amount of which should be determined in the original contract.

9.49   For his part, the au pair must undertake services which consist of the accomplishment of certain daily family tasks (art 9 of the agreement). The time spent on these tasks may not exceed five hours per day.

Finally, the signatory states must also guarantee the au pair medical services in case of sickness, pregnancy or accident (*ibid*, art 10).

(f) Commercial professions

9.50   A Law dated 28 December 1988 concerning the admission to skilled, commercial and industrial professions and to certain liberal professions, hereinafter referred to as the "Establishment Law'," partly governs the matter.

Neither a private person nor a company, regardless of nationality, can either exercise any industrial, commercial or skilled profession or the profession of architect, engineer, chartered accountant or consultant in intellectual property (*propriété industrielle*) without written authorisation from the Minister of the Middle Classes (*Ministère des Classes Moyennes*) after an administrative enquiry and on the advice of a special commission (arts 1 and 2 of the Establishment Law).

The ministerial decisions concerning the grant, the refusal or the revocation of the authorisation can be appealed before the administrative jurisdiction (*Conseil d'Etat*) (*ibid*, art 2). Authorisation can only be granted to a person if they present the necessary guarantees of respectability and professional qualification (*ibid*, art 3).

9.51   With respect to a company, the managers must fulfill the conditions imposed upon the individuals. It is enough that the conditions relative to the professional qualification are fulfilled by the promoter of the company or by the person who is responsible for the management or the direction of the company.

The Law of 27 November 1984, as modified on 1 January 1991, relative to access and surveillance of the financial centre, regulates the establishment of certain credit establishments in the Grand-Duchy of Luxembourg, as well as various other professions, such as asset managers, counsellors in financial operations, fund distributors and brokers/commission agents. The Luxembourg Monetary Institute is competent to supervise the establishment of such entities.

(g) Investors and business persons

9.52   Generally, foreign investors and business persons are subject to the same rules as nationals. In fact, there is in principle no restriction for foreign investors, nor are there any limitations on foreign investment. In practice, most companies which have their registered offices in Luxembourg and which are, therefore, Luxembourg companies have (to a very large extent) shareholders from countries other than Luxembourg. This is understandable, in view of the Luxembourg fiscal legislation, which is rather favourable for non-residents.

With respect to doctors, there is written control of their qualifications **9.53** (verification of their diploma, and the university from which it emanated). With respect to lawyers, there is similarly a control of their diplomas and their professional qualifications. Additionally, there is an obligation to take part in a three year legal internship. (This law is in the process of transformation.)

The Netherlands

Chapter 10
The Netherlands

1. Permanent immigrants

The term "immigrant", being a person who is seeking a new home country for **10.1** permanent residence, is not used in Dutch aliens law. The Dutch Aliens Act of 1965 provides a system of permits for temporary and for permanent stay whereby continued lawful residence on the basis of a temporary residence permit for a period of five years may lead to the acquisition of a permanent residence permit. Imigrants, therefore, may have a temporary residence status.

Visa requirements

As immigrants clearly intend to stay in The Netherlands for more than three **10.2** months, they would generally need to obtain a special visa called *machtiging tot voorlopig verblijf* (authorisation of provisional stay). This special visa is an authorisation to enter and apply for a residence permit for a specific purpose.

The *machtiging tot voorlopig verblijf* should be applied for at the Dutch embassy or consulate in the country where the applicant resides. In case of application for reunion with family, spouse or an unmarried "live in" relation, the family, spouse or "live in" partner concerned may also address the local aliens police. The visa is issued upon authorisation of the Visa Service, a division of the Ministry of Justice, acting on behalf of the Ministry of Foreign Affairs, which is the formal issuing authority of all visas. Most applications are sent to the local aliens police for consultation and advice. The processing of a *machtiging tot voorlopig verblijf* generally takes three to five months.

Immigrants who apply for a residence permit in The Netherlands at the **10.3** office of the local aliens police of the municipality where they have or intend to take up residence, are generally – with exceptions for such reasons as a threat to public order etc – permitted to stay pending the decision upon their application.

As a rule, applications for a residence permit which are made after unauthorised (*i.e.* illegal) entry are rejected. However, jurisprudence has forced the administration to grant a residence permit in spite of non-compliance with visa formalities if it can be said that all requirements for admission have been met by the time the application of the residence permit is actually made. On account of this jurisprudence, the impact of this visa instrument on restrictive policies has been weakened considerably.

Nationals of the following countries are exempted from the obligation to obtain this special visa before entry: Austria, Finland, Iceland, Monaco, Norway, USA, Sweden, Switzerland, and all EC Member States.

(i) **Employment**

(a) **Employees granted work permits**

10.4   Work permits are issued by the Department of Social Affairs and Employment on the basis of the Aliens Employees Act of 1978. The objectives of this Act are:

- restrictive admission of migrant workers;
- improvement of the allocation of jobs on the labour market;
- to fight illegal employment; and
- to warrant freedom of employment to legally residing foreign employees.

10.5   A Bill providing further restrictions on employment by aliens is in preparation. The Dutch cabinet feels that the need for this Bill has come about by the enlargement of the labour market on account of the expansion of the European Community and the creation of a European Economic Area of EC and EFTA countries, by high unemployment rates and by increased labour migration.

All aliens, who are not EC nationals, and who intend to take employment in The Netherlands, must obtain a residence permit and a work permit. The work permit will allow the holder to do the job for which it was granted, but only if, and as long as, he/she is also holding a valid residence permit, issued for the purpose of taking employment.

10.6   A work permit is applied for by the prospective employer at the local employment bureau; the application form requires the signature of the prospective employee. The legal instruction is to decide on an application within 30 days; in practice the processing of a work permit may take four to six weeks. The permit mentions the names of the company and the employee and defines the employment for which it has been granted. For a new position a new work permit is required. In general a work permit is granted for the duration of the contract, but for maximum of three years: after three years the holder becomes eligible for exemption.

10.7   The main criterion for granting a work permit is that the prospective employment by an alien will not injure the interests of the Dutch labour market. Employers have to show that they cannot fill the vacancy with a Dutch or other EC national or with a legal alien. The vacancy should be notified to the local employment bureau prior to the application; candidates referred to the company by the employment bureau should not be turned down without good reason. In suitable cases, the vacancy should also be notified for European recruitment.

Furthermore, employers are supposed to have some awareness of the various avenues for filling vacancies outside the recruitment circuit of the regional employment bureau. For instance they might consider recruiting temporary staff or contracting the work out to a specialist company in The Netherlands. Upon submitting a work permit application, an employer may very well be asked to demonstrate that the vacancy was advertised, not only through the regional employment bureau but also through other appropriate channels.

Companies abroad have to apply for work permits if they intend to have **10.8** their employees working in The Netherlands. This applies also in case of intra-company transfers, involving employees who are being moved from a position with a parent or sister company abroad to a position with a parent or sister company in The Netherlands. Senior managers or personnel with technical skills which are rare in The Netherlands, will have no difficulty in obtaining a work permit.

Having a shareholding in the company does not exempt the employee from the requirement to hold a work permit.

Artists, musicians and models who are contracted to perform in The **10.9** Netherlands also need work permits; in most cases these permits are granted easily.

The age requirements for work permits are as follows:
– for skilled labour: from 18 to 45;
– for unskilled labour: from 18 to 35.

Furthermore, adequate housing should be available for the prospective employee.

(b) Permit-free employment

Most legal aliens are exempted from the work permit requirement. The **10.10** following categories are mentionable:
– EC nationals who have come to The Netherlands to take employment;
– holders of a convention refugee status or a residence permit by way of asylum;
– holders of a permanent residence permit;
– holders of a dependant residence status on account of marriage, family ties or an unmarried relation;
– those who have had lawful employment for three consecutive years;
– those who have their main residence abroad and work in The Netherlands incidentally: repair and maintenance mechanics, prop-men for exhibitions, performers of fine art, foreign militaries, household staff of tourists, au pairs, correspondents, lecturers visiting for less than six months, professional drivers, sportsmen, trainees (on account of treaty provisions);
– those employed by international organisations;
– civil servants;
– seamen on Dutch seagoing vessels.

Proof of exemption is issued upon request to: **10.11**
– refugees and holders of asylum status;
– holders of a permanent residence permit;
– holders of a dependant residence status on account of marriage, family ties or an unmarried relation;
– those who have had lawful (self) employment for three consecutive years.

Proof of exemption takes the form of a white plastic card and must be **10.12** applied for at the local employment bureau. The card is valid only in case of lawful residence. For practical reasons the Dutch cabinet intends to replace the plastic card by a note to be placed in the alien's passport.

(c) Illegal employment

10.13 An employer who illegally employs aliens commits an economic offence, punishable with a prison sentence and a maximum fine of ƒ10,000. In practice the fine is between ƒ750 and ƒ1,250 per illegal employee. It is intended to raise these tariffs to ƒ2,000 and ƒ10,000. The maximum fine will be raised to ƒ100,000.

In this respect it should be mentioned, that the actual employer and not the employment agency should be the holder of a work permit. Investigation is carried out by the local police force and the officials of the Labour Inspection Service (*Dienst Inspectie Arbeidsverhoudingen* (DIA)).

The residence permit of an alien who is working without the required work permit may be withdrawn.

(ii) Business

10.14 The policies on the admission of business persons and professionals are neither extensive nor detailed and jurisprudence on the subject is not abundant.

The key requirement is that the intended activities of the applicant in The Netherlands will serve essential Dutch economic interests. Of course, the other requirement would be that the applicant will earn a sufficient income in this way. It is difficult to say which activities may be "essential" in this context and which may not. Many related factors may be relevant, like the qualifications, expertise and experience of the applicant, the expected profit, the number of Dutch nationals or legal aliens to be employed, the amount of the investment, the extent to which there will be competition with settled business in The Netherlands.

10.15 Applications for an authorisation of provisionary stay or a residence permit must be accompanied by satisfactory documentation giving details of the expected future turnover and profit and by an explanation why it would be necessary for the applicant to reside in The Netherlands to pursue his business or professional activities.

The exploitation of restaurants and the like is licensed and conditional on professional qualifications. The same goes for most branches of the retail trade, but in some cases exemptions are granted. Professionals like doctors, pharmacists and craftsmen must have qualifications which match Dutch standards. All applications are decided upon by the Aliens Department of the Ministry of Justice acting upon the advice of the Ministry of Economic Affairs.

10.16 Writers, artists and musicians may obtain a residence permit if their intended activities in The Netherlands can be considered to serve essential Dutch cultural or artistic interests. In most cases it is impossible to predict whether or not someone will meet this requirement; the Aliens Department decides after consultation with the Ministry of Culture.

Applications from foreign seamen who have been working on Dutch ships or drilling platforms for seven years consecutively, who have a good record and are still under 60 years of age, are exempted from the "Dutch essential interests" requirement.

(iii) Persons of independent means/investors

10.17 The purchase of real estate (land, houses, industrial complexes), making investments (industrial development, restaurants, shops) or buying shares in domestic companies, is not in itself a ground for granting a residence permit. The one exception may be conduct of business by United States citizens, who have made a considerable investment or intend to do so, as mentioned in Article II of the American–Dutch Friendship Treaty of 27 March 1956.

Taking up residence on the basis of investments or for the purpose of retirement is restricted by the "Dutch essential interests" requirement: applicants must show a need for their presence in the public interest. In each case it will be considered whether some essential Dutch interest would require the applicant to stay in The Netherlands for a longer period than would be possible on the basis of a visitor's or business visa. This may be particularly difficult for investors who would only want to be involved financially and could act through an agent or proxy.

10.18 Retirement, to live on one's private means will only very rarely be considered to serve essential Dutch interests, and will generally not constitute compelling humanitarian grounds for granting a residence permit. For recently published policies on the admission of elderly people as a form of extended family reunion, see para 9.27 of this chapter.

In the cases of US citizens the policies on admission for retirement seem to be less strict every now and then, perhaps on account of the American–Dutch Friendship Treaty, but much depends on the particulars of the application.

(iv) Family and marriage

10.19 Family life is protected both by national and international law. Article 10 of the Dutch Constitution protects everybody's private life of which family life may very well be a part. Article 8 of the European Convention on the protection of Human Rights (ECHR) and article 23 of the International Covenant on Civil and Political Rights explicitly protect family life. Jurisprudence has made article 8 ECHR a cornerstone of Dutch aliens law.

Paragraph 1 of article 8 grants everybody the elementary human right to family life. Paragraph 2 explicitly stipulates non interference with this right by any public authority "except such as is in accordance with the law and is necessary in a democratic society in the interests of national security, public safety or the economic well-being of the country, for the prevention of disorder or crime, for the protection of health or morals, or the protection of the rights and freedoms of others." The elements of this clause are frequently used by the Department of Justice for refusing family life applications and turning down petitions for administrative review.

10.20 In 1985 the European Court of Justice in Strasbourg ruled that family life comprises a relation based on a lawful and sincere marriage, notwithstanding the fact that the spouses are not yet living together. In 1988 the Court ruled that the relation of a divorced Moroccan father and his daughter, who were in contact with each other four times a week for a couple of hours, constitutes family life notwithstanding the fact that they were not actually living together as members of one family.

So the criterion appears to be that the alien involved is keeping actual family ties rather than family ties in strict terms of family law. In Dutch jurisprudence several factors are taken into account: the age of the child(ren), the frequency, duration and character of the contacts, whether these contacts have been judicially endorsed, whether the foreign parent supports his child(ren) financially and if so, to what demonstrable extent.

10.21   There is no interference with family life if the family member(s) in The Netherlands can reasonably be expected to accmpany the alien abroad.

The answer to the question whether an infringement of family life is justifiable results from an evaluation of both the public interest and the interest which the persons involved may have in maintaining and continuing their family life in The Netherlands. Generaly speaking, in cases of first admission the national interests of the state with regard to the economic well-being will outweigh the individual interests.

10.22   Family admissions are of two kinds:
(i)   family reunion: – regular
                                             – partial
                                             – extended
(ii)   family formation: – getting married
                                             – starting an unmarried "live in" relationship
                                             – taking a foreign foster-child.

(a) Family reunion

10.23   Holders of a residence permit who intend to be joined by their spouse and children must have sufficient and durable financial means and adequate housing. "Sufficient" is a net income equal to the social benefit standard for a married couple pursuant to the General Social Security Act (ABW): f1760,31 monthly as per 1 January 1993. "Durable income" is income which will be earned for at least another year.

Housing should be adequate in the opinion of the municipal housing authorities, *i.e.* be acceptable for Dutch families in similar circumstances. Standards can be found in municipal by-laws on building.

10.24   Regular family reunion concerns the spouse and children under 18, who are de facto living in the family. Jurisprudence has accepted that children may have been raised in a family structure different from the regular Western pattern. However, family life is restricted to one partner and the children born from that relationship. In case of polygamy, the alien must make a choice. A man, having an unmarried "live in" relation in The Netherlands, cannot be joined by his legal spouse and children. Whether children were born in or out of wedlock, is irrelevant. It may occur, that one of the children reaches the age of 18 while the head of the family is still awaiting adequate housing. This child will qualify nevertheless if he is under 23, not married, was part of the family in the homeland, is dependent on the head of the family and has arrived with the other members of the family whilst the head of the family was registered with the local Housing Department as a house hunter by the time he became 18.

Partial family reunion, with the spouse and/or some of the children, is **10.25** possible if all requirements for reunion of the whole family have been met. However, the risk for those who may come later is evident; the Department of Justice may take the view that actual family ties have ceased to exist in the meantime.   Arriving later on account of military service in the homeland will be accepted, if the applicant was under 18 at the time the other family members arrived, and applies to enter The Netherlands within six months after termination of his service. The same term applies for the readmission of those who have to leave their family to perform military services in the homeland.

Extended family reunion concerns members of the family other than spouse **10.26** and children. Requirements are, that they were actually part of the family in the homeland, that they are both financially and morally dependent on the head of the family and that it would be disproportionately hard to leave them behind. The Dutch Aliens Circular mentions in this respect needy parents (in law) and unmarried daughters of age. Jurisprudence has allowed divorced women who are socially isolated to join their former family in cases of severe hardship.

In November 1991 criteria for the admission of elderly parents and **10.27** grandparents were published.

Applicants of 65 and over may be admitted if:
- they are socially isolated in their homeland;
- (practically) all their children live in The Netherlands and are permanent residents or Dutch citizens;
- the children, either one or all together, have sufficient means to keep their parent;
- adequate housing is available: the parent should live with or in the vicinity of the child(ren);
- they do not pose a risk to the public peace.

For Dutch nationals, permanent residents and convention refugees, the **10.28** financial requirements for family reunion have been mitigated: only reproachable unemployment constitutes a ground for refusal. However, there seems to be a political consensus within the Dutch cabinet to bring about changes in this respect.

Dutch nationals and convention refugees are also exempted from the adequate housing requirement.

Health insurance is obligatory in all cases of family reunion.

(b) Family formation

In case of marriage with the holder of a residence permit, criteria for admission **10.29** are the same as for regular family reunion. In case of marriage with a Dutch national, permanent resident or convention refugee, the same mitigated requirements as mentioned above are applicable.

The spouses may have been married abroad or in The Netherlands; in all cases the marriage should be valid according to the rules of Dutch international family law. The spouses should live at the same address and share a common household, or have the intention to do so. Recently two bills were sent to parliament to oppose sham marriages.

10.30   Admission on account of an unmarried "live in" relationship is also possible. The nature of the relationship, hetero- or homosexual, is irrelevant. The partner already living in The Netherlands must be either Dutch or an EC national, a permanent resident or a convention refugee. The specific criteria are as follows. The partners should have a lasting relationship: they live together and share a common household. Both partners should be unmarried unless one of them is not able to obtain a divorce. The partner of the applicant should have sufficient means to take full financial responsibility for the cost of living and eventual return of the applicant to the homeland. Normally, if there is a lack of sufficient means, a guarantee from friends or relatives will be acceptable. Finally, housing should be adequate.

10.31   Taking a foreign foster-child can be done in two ways. First, there are admissions of foster-children with the explicit intention of adoption according to the rules and procedures of Dutch family law. If a – not necessarily Dutch – couple has satisfied all the requirements laid down in the Act on the Adoption of Foreign Foster-children, admission will be granted. After adoption later on, the child will automatically become a Dutch citizen if one of the foster-parents is Dutch.

Secondly, there are admissions of foreign children who will not be adopted, but who are taken into the family by next of kin because of their parent's inability to care for them. Less prosperous living conditions as such do not constitute "inability".

2. Visitors, students and temporary workers

10.32   This this section the word "visitor" is used in connection with the word "immigrant." An immigrant being any person seeking a new home country for permanent residence, a visitor is regarded as a person seeking temporary stay or residence for a specific purpose.

Visa requirements

(a) Temporary stay up to a maximum of three months

10.33   In general, visas are required for short term stays to a maximum of three months under article 8 of the Aliens Act.

Visa requirements mainly result from the Benelux Agreement on the Transfer of Control of Persons to the External Borders of the Benelux

Territory. According to this Agreement of 1960 the Benelux has become a common travel area; a Benelux visa is valid for the Benelux territory.

Citizens of most non-European countries must show a valid passport and a visa upon entry at the border. Since 1960 The Netherlands, Belgium and Luxembourg have had a common policy regarding visas; a Benelux visa is valid for the Benelux territory.

A list of countries whose nationals do not require a visa for short term stay **10.34** under article 8 of the Aliens Act is set out in the Appendix at the end of this chapter. Nationals of the twelve EC Member States are also exempt from the requirement for a visa under EC law. It is expected that the list of those who do not require a visa will be completely revised in the near future, after the implementation of the provisions of the Schengen Agreements.

The Schengen Agreements of 1985 and 1990 have been signed by the Benelux countries, France, Germany, Italy, Portugal and Spain. In view of the achievement of a single European market in 1993 whereby the internal European borders will be abolished, these countries have agreed on a common system of controls at the external borders of their territory. The Schengen provisions provide, amongst other things, for a common policy on visas and a uniform visa for the Schengen territory, much like the actual Benelux visa.

Benelux visas can be applied for at the embassy or consulate of The Netherlands, Belgium or Luxembourg abroad. Visa applications may be dealt with at the diplomatic post or may be sent to the Visa Service (*Visadienst*) of the Ministry of Foreign Affairs in The Hague for investigation and instructions; the visa policies pursuant to the Benelux Agreement on the Transfer of Control of Persons to the External Borders of the Benelux Territory are not published. As a consequence, visa applications can take anything from a few hours to a few months.

Visas for short-term stay are issued for a period of up to a maximum of three months. Extensions can be applied for at the local aliens police up to the maximum period of six months. The validity of the visa is linked to the validity of the passport and the return ticket.

A visa is no guarantee that admission will be granted; those with visas are **10.35** still required to hold a valid passport and to have sufficient financial means to support themselves, and these conditions will be checked upon entry at the border. A visa can be annulled if a visitor fails to comply with any of these conditions, if he is registered as an alien, excluded from entry, or if he apparently intends to take up residence.

Those who need to visit The Netherlands frequently for business purposes **10.36** can obtain a so-called business visa. This visa grants multiple entry for a stay of up to a total of 30 days within a 6 or 12 month period.

Aliens in possession of a residence permit or other valid title of permitted stay have a right to enter The Netherlands at all times.

(b) Temporary stay exceeding three months

A special visa, called *machtiging tot voorlopig verblijf* (authorisation of provisional **10.37** stay) is required for temporary stay exceeding three months: it authorises an alien to come to The Netherlands and apply for a residence permit.

An authorisation of provisional stay should be applied for at the Dutch embassy or consulate in the country where the applicant lives or resides. The visa is issued upon authorisation of the Visa Service, a division of the Ministry of Justice, acting on behalf of the Ministry of Foreign Affairs, which is the formal issuing authority of all visas. Most applications are sent to the local aliens police for consultation and advice. The processing of an authorisation of provisional stay generally takes three to five months.

10.38   Imigrants who apply for a residence permit in The Netherlands at the office of the local aliens police of the municipality where they have or intend to take up residence, are generally – with exceptions for such reasons as a threat to public order etc – permitted to stay pending the decision upon their application. As a rule, applications for a residence permit which are made after unauthorised (*i.e.* illegal) entry are rejected. However, jurisprudence has forced the administration to grant a residence permit in spite of non-compliance with visa formalities if it can be said that all requirements for admission have been met by the time the aplication for the residence permit is actually made. On account of this jurisprudence, the impact of this visa instrument on restrictive policies has been weakened considerably.

Nationals of the following countries are exempted from the obligation to obtain this special visa before entry: Austria, Finland, Iceland, Monaco, Norway, USA, Sweden, Switzerland and all EC Member States.

(i) Tourists and family visitors

10.39   For a tourist or family visit which lasts for no longer than three months, a valid passport is required and sufficient funds to finance the intended period of stay and the cost of the return journey. Immigration officers carefully check on funds and return tickets. Visitors, or their guarantors, may be required to deposit funds with the immigration authorities. These funds are returned upon departure. Problems may be avoided by showing a letter of invitation from a relative or a friend who is willing to act as guarantor for the cost of the intended period of stay and the return journey. It is also advisable to be in possession of a return ticket.

Aliens entering on a visa, are instructed to report to the local aliens police within two days; aliens exempted from visa obligations have to report within eight days. Those staying in a hotel only have to fill in a form.

(ii) Business visitors

10.40   Visitors for business purposes, self-employed persons such as traders and investors, may be admitted for a maximum period of three months for transacting business during their visit. However, as the occasion arises, they should make clear that the business intended cannot be considered as seeking self-employment with the intention of taking up residence, *i.e.* for a stay of more than three months.

Business persons, who have been admitted as short-term stay visitors but who have changed their mind later on and clearly intend to take up residence (they, for example, rent an office and register their business with the Chamber of Commerce) should report to the local aliens police within eight days and apply for a residence permit.

The key requirement for admission is that the intended activities will serve **10.41** essential Dutch interests. Many factors can be relevant, like the amount of the investment, the qualifications and experience of the applicant, the expected profit or the number of Dutch nationals and/or legal aliens to be employed. Furthermore, the extent of expected competition with companies already settled in The Netherlands may be important.

All applications are dealt with by the Aliens Department of the Ministry of Justice acting upon the advice of the Ministry of Economic Affairs.

(iii) Temporary workers, working holidaymakers and intra-company transfers

According to the Aliens Employees Act, any alien coming to The Netherlands **10.42** for the purpose of taking gainful employment needs to obtain a work permit through his prospective employer. Employers in The Netherlands and abroad are forbidden to employ aliens in The Netherlands without a work permit. However, an application for a work permit will not be dealt with if the prospective employee has not previously obtained or applied for a residence permit to take up this employment. Therefore, short-term stay visitors who have come with the clear intention to work for not more than three months consecutively, should apply for a residence permit within eight days after arrival in order to submit an admissible application for a work permit.

Intra-company transfers may take place within multinational companies **10.43** with offices in different countries or within any other international chain of companies related by economics or jurisdiction. Foreign functionaries who are to be transferred to the Dutch division, settlement, branch and the like should obtain a residence permit for gainful employment and a work permit for the prospective job. Senior managers or personnel with technical skills which are rare in The Netherlands will have no difficulty in obtaining a work permit. Usually the residence permit will be granted soon after the issue of the work permit.

(iv) Students

For studies of up to three months foreign students must comply with the same **10.44** requirements as other foreign visitors; they need a valid passport, sufficient funds and, depending on their nationality, a visa.

For studies which take more than three months a foreign student must:
-   produce proof of matriculation at a university, college or educational institution;
-   sign a statement that he/she is aware of the fact that admission has been granted for purposes of study only; and

- have sufficient funds to finance the cost of the intended study and the cost of living.

10.45   Admission for study is only granted for full-time educational courses. Studies at a university or polytechnic college (third degree) should not be intended for employment in The Netherlands. For studies at secondary level and vocational courses The Netherlands should be the most suitable country. This criterion is vague, but means that the intended study or course should not be available in the student's home country. Furthermore, the intended study or course should enable the student to contribute to the development of his home country.

10.46   For preparatory studies (*e.g.* Dutch language) a residence permit can be obtained for up to a maximum of one year. It should be mentioned that the period of one year for preparatory studies is not calculated from the date of application but from the date of entry.

Aliens who obtained a residence permit to study are not permitted to take employment unless the work can be regarded as practice and a work permit – if needed – has been granted.

10.47   A foreign student can be accompanied by his spouse and children. They will receive a depandant residence permit. Sufficient funds and adequate housing should be available.

Permission to stay will cease upon completion or termination of studies or if the study is considered to have taken too long.

(v) **Scholars**

10.48   As for all aliens in general, criteria for the admission of scholars depend on the duration and the purpose of the intended stay. Visiting lecturers, for example, may be admitted for a maximum period of three months under the conditions and restrictions of article 8 Aliens Act, much like business visitors. Scholars who have come to The Netherlands as visiting lecturers at a Dutch institution for academic education (university etc) for lecturing up to a maximum of six months, are exempted from the requirement to have obtained a work permit.

10.49   Foreign scholars who intend to conduct scientific research during their visit must obtain a work permit. As has been mentioned before (see paras 10.33–10.38) in cases like these research scholars should apply for a residence permit, even for short-term activities of less than three months.

(vi) **Au pairs**

10.50   Residence as an au pair serves a cultural purpose. Young people are given the opportunity to stay with a host family in The Netherlands and gain an introduction to Dutch society in this way. Household work by an au pair is admissible and exempted from the work permit requirement.

10.51   An au pair:
- is between 18 and 30 years of age;
- has to sign a statement that he/she is aware of the fact that admission has been granted for au pair purposes only;

- has to sign a statement that he/she has no criminal record;
- will be admitted for a maximum period of one year, but can switch to another host family within this year.

The head of the host family has to sign a guarantor statement for the cost of living and return to the home country of the au pair. Health insurance is obligatory.

3. **Refugees and political asylum**

Dutch policies distinguish between invited refugees and individual refugees. **10.52** Invited refugees are recognised as such by the Dutch government; they are transferred to The Netherlands on behalf of the government, usually upon the request of the United Nations High Commissioner for Refugees (UNHCR); they number 750 per year.

Article 15 of the Aliens Act defines a refugee as a person with a well-founded **10.53** fear of persecution for religious or political convictions, nationality or because he belongs to a certain race or social group. This concept is identical to the one that has been defined in article 1A(2) of the Convention Relating to the Status of Refugees: the Refugee Convention of Geneva (1951). Article 33 of the convention embodies the principle of *non refoulement* which has direct effect in Dutch aliens law: those who claim to be refugees will not be refused entry and will not be deported, unless by special leave from the Minister of Justice. Both asylum seekers and convention refugees are protected by this principle. Asylum applications are decided by the Aliens Affairs Department of the Ministry of Justice.

(i) **Recent developments**

As the existing asylum procedure proved insufficient to cope with the **10.54** increasing numbers of individual applicants, a new procedure has become operational in the course of 1992, which should be both humane and efficient for the 20,000 applicants per year. The new procedure has been designed to bring about an important acceleration in the processing of asylum applications. The main features of the new procedure are:

- to refuse entry to and detain asylum seekers reporting at any port of entry at the border;
- to differentiate at an early stage between those asylum applications which are to succeed and those which are not;
- to grant limited possibilities for legal remedy to those who have been refused and to restrict their freedom of movement until their actual – if necessary forced – departure from the country.

In view of these features, it is questionable whether the new procedure meets **10.55** the internationally accepted standards for asylum procedures, formulated in the conclusions of the United Nations High Commissioner for Refugees and the recommendations of the Committee of Ministers of the Council of Europe.

In the European context the Dutch procedure is anticipating the approaching operation of the Schengen Agreements. The EC Convention of Dublin on determining the state responsible for examining asylum requests (June 1990, not ratified yet by all EC Member States) should also be mentioned. In the forthcoming European system an alien will be allowed to make an asylum application in one Member State only; only one Member State will be responsible for examining the request. The Schengen Information System (SIS) will warrant the operation of this "one application in Europe" principle.

10.56 An *ad hoc* group on immigration advising the EC Council of Ministers is preparing recommendations on the application and implementation of the Dublin Convention, on harmonisation of substantive asylum law, on harmonisation of expulsion policies, on setting up a clearing house, on legal examination and on the conditions for receiving applicants for asylum.

10.57 At the Conference of the Ministers of Justice of the EC Member States in Lisbon on 12 June 1992, draft conclusions were adopted on common asylum policies in Europe. The Member States have committed themselves to adapt their national legislations as far as necesary in order to start carrying out these conclusions before 1 July 1994. One of the conclusions contains an extensive interpretation of the "country of first refuge principle": asylum seekers who have been travelling to Europe through a "safe" non-European country, will be sent back to this country of first refuge. Criteria for "safety" should be in conformity with the *non refoulement* principle laid down in the Geneva Refugee Convention of 1951.

10.58 Jurisprudence on asylum upheld the policy by which a special status was created for aliens, who reasonably cannot be expected to return to their home country in view of the prevailing conditions of life there. This so-called C-status can be considered as an implementation of the Dutch government's humanitarian policies. It takes the form of an unrestricted residence permit.

By the end of 1991 the Dutch parliament agreed to a new policy by which a status *extra legem* has been created. Asylum seekers who are considered not to qualify for any type of residence permit, but who cannot be deported to their home country in view of the prevailing conditions of life there (civil war, natural catastrophies etc), are permitted to stay in The Netherlands for the time being. In the meantime any procedure pending to obtain a regular title of permitted stay will be suspended. However, if after three and a half years the asylum seeker cannot be deported, a C-status will be granted. So far, this status *extra legem* has not been tested in the courts.

Since July 1992 special policies have been pursued with regard to asylum seekers from the former Yugoslavia. According to a Temporary Relief Arrangement, applicants are provided with food, shelter and some pocket-money; they are not allowed to work. Their applications for asylum are suspended. As of 13 April 1993 the Dutch Government has started to settle these cases. Newcomers from Slovenia, Croatia, Macedonia and The Federal Republic of Serbia and Montenegro will no longer be accepted under the

Temporary Relief Arrangement, which will be effective until 1 January 1994 but will be extended if it is considered necessary.

(ii) The new asylum application procedure

Immigration officers are obliged to give information about the Dutch asylum application procedure to any alien indicating that upon refusal of entry to or expulsion from The Netherlands he would be forced to return to a country where he has a well-founded fear of persecution.   **10.59**

Aliens requesting asylum at a port of entry may be refused entry; pending a first decision they will be detained in a Reception and Investigation Centre anywhere in the country. Asylum seekers arriving at Schiphol Airport have been receiving this treatment for some years already. In the beginning they were held for a considerable time in the transit area; nowadays they are accommodated in a newly built detention centre on the outskirts of Amsterdam.

Asylum seekers who report to the local aliens police are referred for application to one of nine Reception and Investigation Centres spread nationwide. All inhabitants of asylum centres receive an identity document and must report regularly to the aliens police.   **10.60**

The application comprises recognition and admission as a convention refugee or admission on the basis of a regular residence permit for humanitarian reasons. A first decision will be processed within 30 days on the basis of an interview with a liaison officer of the Ministry of Justice. A few days are granted for the applicant to prepare for the interview; legal aid and qualified interpreters are available. The applicant will be interviewed about the particulars of his journey to The Netherlands and all relevant facts and circumstances which caused him to leave his homeland. It is very important for the applicant to produce documentation to substantiate and account for the credibility of his statements.

Manifestly ill-founded requests will be rejected with recourse only to the President of the District Court in The Hague, to be addressed within 24 hours, in order to initiate summary proceedings for obtaining an injunction order against deportation pending administrative review. Those asylum seekers will be restricted in their freedom of movement until their actual deportation or voluntary departure, unless, of course, they would win their case in court.   **10.61**

Those who are likely to be admitted are subsequently accommodated in a regular Reception Centre for a maximum period of six months in order to finalise the application procedure and make arrangements for their settlement in society.

Refugees are granted a permanent and unrestricted residence permit; they are entitled to a Convention Travel Document. Refugee status can be withdrawn if circumstances have changed to the effect that the alien can take up residence outside The Netherlands without risking persecution.   **10.62**

4. Permanent residence and nationality

(i) Permanent residence

10.63   An alien may be entitled to a permanent residence permit after five years of lawful residence in The Netherlands, from the age of thirteen. "Lawful" in this respect means: holding a residence permit or family member status. The requirements are:
- financial means, both sufficient and durable; and
- no serious infringements of national security or public peace.

The aliens police is instructed to properly inform any alien, who may be entitled to a permanent residence permit, about his rights in this respect. Sufficient financial means is a net income equal to the minimum income benefit pursuant to the standards of the General Social Security Act (ABW): ƒ1760,31 monthly as of 1 January 1993.

10.64   Aliens:
- who have been residing legally in The Netherlands for five years consecutively; and
- who are living in wedlock or in an unmarried "live in" relationship with a Dutch national or legal alien who is earning a standard family income according to the ABW

are exempted from the financial means criterion. This policy has been adopted in the interests of foreign women who have no job and are living at home. Disablement Insurance Act (WAO) benefits based on an incapacitation percentage of 55 or more, are also considered as sufficient financial means. Second generation aliens, admitted for family life before the age of 13, are entitled to a permanent residence permit without financial requirements when they become 18.

Legal aliens who qualified for a permanent residence permit in the past, will be granted a permit without further financial requirements.

10.65   Financial means must be durable. For this criterion the applicant's job and social benefits record is taken into account. Jobs which started less than one year ago and offer no prospect of lasting for at least another year, are not durable. Aliens, admitted for temporary purposes such as study or medical treatment, do not qualify for a permanent residence permit, because they are considered not to have a durable income.

An applicant will be exempted from the financial means criterion after 10 years of lawful residence.

10.66   Financial factors cannot lead to withdrawal of a residence permit.

A permanent residence permit is valid indefinitely but is considered to have terminated *ipso iure* after voluntary absence from The Netherlands for nine months or more. In these cases, it is up to the alien to prove that his absence was involuntary.

(ii) **Nationality**

Article 2 of the Dutch Constitution says that the law will determine who is a **10.67**
Dutch citizen. This constitutional order has been carried out in the Dutch
Citizenship Act of 1985 (*Rijkswet op het Nederlanderschap*).

Dutch citizenship may be acquired (a) by descent, (b) by choice (option)
and (c) by naturalisation.

(a) Descent

Children of a Dutch father or mother are Dutch by birth. Children who do not **10.68**
have a Dutch parent but who have a Dutch grandmother who was living in
The Netherlands at the time their parent was born, are Dutch by birth as well,
provided that this parent was living in The Netherlands when this child was
born. In these cases, the place of birth of the child is in no way relevant.

(b) Choice (option)

By deposition of a simple statement of option at the local town hall, Dutch **10.69**
embassy or consulate, this option is open to aliens between 18 and 25 who have
been living in The Netherlands since they were born.

Women who lost Dutch nationality by marriage before 1 January 1985 can
reclaim it by deposition of a statement of option within one year of their
divorce or the death of their spouse.

(c) Naturalisation

Dutch citizenship will be granted if the applicant has met the following **10.70**
requirements:
(i)   the applicant should be 18 years of age or over;
(ii)   there should be no objection to permanent residence in The Netherlands
      or in the Dutch Antilles; this will generally imply that one should have a
      permanent residence status (*e.g.* students and those staying for medical
      treatment do not qualify);
(iii)   the applicant should have lived permanently in the Kingdom (The
      Netherlands and the Dutch Antilles) immediately prior to the applica-
      tion.
      The following categories are exempted from this requirement:
      – former Dutch citizens, such as Surinam nationals: they are not
         required to have lived in the Kingdom for any specific term;
      – partners of Dutch spouses or those in an unmarried "live in"
         relationship with a Dutch national, are required to have lived in the
         Kingdom for a period of three years instead of five.
(iv)   the applicant should have assimilated with Dutch society, which means
      that he should have an acceptable command of the Dutch language and
      have adapted to Dutch society. There is ample jurisprudence on the
      language criterion. A system of approved certificates has not been
      introduced yet;

(v)   the applicant should pose no danger to public peace and/or public security;

(vi)   until recently it was required that the applicant should have taken all necessary steps to renounce his former nationality, unless this would be unreasonable: *e.g.* nationals from Greece, Morocco, Tunisia, Iran and East European countries have no legal possibility of renouncing their nationality. This policy, adopted in the interest of preventing dual nationality, has been abandoned; renouncing nationality has now become optional.

10.71   Children under the age of 18 participate in the naturalisation of either one of their parents. However, children living abroad may be excluded.

5. Discretion

10.72   Rules and regulations concerning immigration are enforced by the Royal Dutch Military Police and customs officers at the border, by the local aliens police and by the officials of the Aliens Department of the Ministry of Justice, headed by the State Secretary of Justice. All of them have separate responsibilities.

The wide discretionary powers, which were given to these authorities in the Aliens Act, are specified and restricted in a set of administrative rules called the Aliens Circular (*Vreemdelingen Circulaire*). These rules have a certain statutory force resulting from the principle that similar cases should be dealt with similarly. Decisions contrary to the rules laid out in the Aliens Circular are permissible only if they favour the alien.

10.73   The Circular on Border Control of 1984 contains administrative rules which have been formulated as instructions from the Minister of Justice to the Royal Dutch Military Police and customs officers.

The general supervision and the final, policial, responsibility for the implementation of Dutch aliens law rest with the State Secretary of Justice.

6. Sanctions

(i) Deportation

10.74   Deportation may be defined as involuntary removal of an alien from Dutch territory. Aliens who do not have permission to stay (anymore) qualify for deportation. Aliens to whom entry has been refused, are put back on an aircraft, train or ship owned by the company which transported the alien to The Netherlands. If removal must be carried out in another way, the costs thereof will be passed on to the transport company. Those who claim to be rufugees are not refused entry and will not be deported unless by special leave of the Minister of Justice.

Deportation is carried out by order of the Minister of Justice or the local aliens police. The order is given in writing to the officer or official in charge of the deportation. The legal intention of the order is to warrant a justifiable deportation of aliens who, in some way, have been staying legally in the country. **10.75**

In cases of illegal entry and/or stay any alien can be deported without a deportation order (with exceptions including EC nationals).

Before carrying out a deportation order, the officer or official in charge must grant the alien a reasonable term (often two weeks) to prepare his departure to a country where entry is warranted. The Supreme Court has ruled that this entry does not have to warrant (taking up) residence. **10.76**

A reasonable term for voluntary departure may be refused in case of illegal entry to The Netherlands, well-founded fear that the alien might go into hiding or other circumstances which will prevent entry or transit elsewhere if deportation is delayed, or in case of a serious criminal or doubtful political record.

However, all aliens who are deported are free to choose a country of destination; they must demonstrate that entry is warranted and pay for the travel expenses. In other cases the costs of the deportation will be passed on to the alien if he has financial means, or to eventual guarantors. **10.77**

To carry out a deportation order or a remand in custody, border officials and aliens police officers are authorised to search houses and other places with a warrant.

Family members, who qualify for deportation, will be enabled to travel together as far as possible.

The deportation of aliens frequently poses problems to the authorities. In many cases a country prepared to give leave for entry cannot be found, mostly because the alien's nationality cannot be verified. **10.78**

The approaching operation of the Schengen Agreements will oblige the Dutch authorities to make arrangements for deportation of alients out of the Schengen territory.

Deportation will not be carried out, as a matter of right or by policy as long as: **10.79**
- the alien is allowed to stay on the basis of a residence title mentioned in the Aliens Act;
- a deportation order, if required, is not given;
- the reasonable term for voluntary departure has not expired;
- the deportation should be postponed considering the health of the persons to be deported;
- criminal prosecution is proceeding or punishment for criminal offences is executed;
- in anticipation of a request for extradition from a foreign authority;
- the applicant is allowed to stay pending the decision of the District Court in The Hague in a procedure to determine Dutch citizenship;

  –   the applicant is allowed to stay, either by right or by policy, pending an application procedure with regard to a residence title, a procedure of administrative review or an appeal to the Judicial Division of the Council of State.

10.80   Problems may arise if deportation can be carried out only to a country where the alien concerned will be prosecuted or subjected to punishment for criminal offences, where extradition cannot or will not be requested. By lack of any alternative, deportation will be carried out, but without previous warning to the authorities of the state of destination or any other contact which might alert them. In 1963 the Supreme Court did not disqualify such deportation as "disguised extradition"; under the circumstances of the case the deportation was considered to be "reasonably necessary" (Dutch Jurisprudence, NJ 1963, 509).

    Stay of execution pending applications, review and appeals, is in many cases the object of a claim in summary proceedings with the President of the District Court in The Hague. By policy, deportation will not be carried out pending the decision of the President.

(ii) Detention

10.81   Deprivation of liberty under the Aliens Act is permitted for:
  –   holding for interrogation to assess identity and residence title;
  –   aliens detention.

    An alien can be held in a police station for interrogation for a maximum of six hours, with the exception of the hours between midnight and 9.00 am. On well-founded suspicion of illegal stay, an alien can be held for another 48 hours.

10.82   Detention can be executed in the interest of public peace or national security if:
  –   a deportation order is given;
  –   a deportation order is likely to be given; or
  –   the application for a residence permit by an illegal alien is likely to be turned down.

    Without a deportation order the maximum duration of detention is one month (30 days). For detention based on a deportation order there is no maximum duration fixed by law; according to the jurisprudence of the District Courts this form of aliens' detention may last up to about seven months. Detention should not be executed or should be stopped, if and as soon as the alien concerned expresses his will to leave the country and demonstrates actual means to carry out this plan (passport, ticket, money, warranted entry).

10.83   A detention order is given by the head of the local aliens police or an officer with the rank of substitute public prosecutor. The order will not be given without interrogation of the alien concerned. This interrogation is covered with several guarantees, both by law and by jurisprudence. The alien has the right to have a lawyer present for assistance and he should be informed about this right by the aliens police officer in charge. If necessary, an interpreter should be involved and an official report of the interrogation should be made.

A request to the District Court to lift the detention, can be made by the alien **10.84** or his lawyer at all times. The court is obliged to hear the alien at least on the first request. The public prosecutor is obliged to inform the court about the detention of any alien which has lasted for 30 days when a request for lifting has not been filed. This notification will be dealt with by the court as if a first request for lifting the order had been made. In case an alien has no lawyer, the court will appoint one.

A request for lifting the order will be granted if the detention is either unlawful or would be – upon consideration of all interests involved – not justifiable anymore. If a request is granted, the court may also grant a claim for damages and compensation.

Although aliens' detention may clearly have a punitive character, it is **10.85** defined as a means of administrative control. The legal system of aliens' detention was designed to match the requirements of article 5 of the European Convention for Human Rights.

Aliens' detention must be carried out in a house of detention after four days. Because most aliens' detentions are carried out in police stations for more than four days, the cabinet has introduced a bill to legalise this practice.

For the detention of juveniles special rules are applicable.

Appendix – Visa exemptions

Nationals of the following countries do not require a visa for entry to The Netherlands.

A10.1

Andorra	Malaysia
Argentina	Malta
Australia	Mexico
	Monaco
Botswana	
Brazil	Nicaragua
Brunei	New Zealand
Burkina-Faso	Nigeria
	Norway
Canada	
Chad	Panama
Chile	Paraguay
Costa Rica	Poland
Cyprus	
	San Marino
Ecuador	Senegal
El Salvador	Singapore
	South Korea
Finland	Swaziland
	Sweden
Guatemala	Switzerland
Honduras	Thailand
	Togo
Iceland	Tunisia
Israel	
Ivory Coast	United States
	Uruguay
Jamaica	
Japan	Vatican City
	Venezuela
Lesotho	
	Yugoslavia
Malawi	

Portugal

Chapter 11
Portugal

Introduction

Country characteristics

The Republic of Portugal occupies an area of slightly more than 92,100 square **11.1**
kilometres in the extreme south-west of Europe. The territory of Portugal
comprises mainland Portugal on the Iberian Peninsula which it shares with
Spain and the Islands of Madeira and Azores in the Atlantic Ocean. The
population is around 10 million and the main cities are Lisbon (1.5 million)
and Oporto (700,000).

The official language is Portuguese which is also spoken in Brazil, Angola,
Mozambique, S. Tomé e Principe, Cape Verde, Guinea Bissau and Macau by
a total of around 200 million people.

Portugal is a founder member of OECD and NATO and since 1986 a full **11.2**
member of the European Community. Membership of the European Community is having a major impact on the economy of Portugal, arising from
easier access to European Markets, the liberalisation of trade and investments, the availability of assistance through EC structural funds and the
pressure on business to modernise in preparation for the single market after
1992. The inflation rate was just over 11% in 1991 and the unemployment
rate in the same period was 5.9%, one of the lowest in the European
Community.

The system of government is a parliamentary democracy. The President of
the Republic is the head of state and represents the nation as whole but the
day-to-day administration of the country rests with the government which is
led by a Prime Minister.

The constitution of 1976 enshrined the fundamental civil rights and public
freedoms and assigned legislative powers to the Parliament and the government, executive power to the government and judicial power to the
courts.

The government's attitude towards immigration

In spite of the existence of laws regulating immigration to Portugal, a **11.3**
considerable degree of discretionary power is held by the Immigration
Authorities. In fact provisions of the law are purposely vague, most of the time
generally referring to guide-lines, leaving its interpretation and application in
the hands of governmental entities which decide on a case by case basis.

145

Therefore, even if from a "written law" point of view, Portuguese legislation may be seen as more favourable to immigrants than other European laws, one must bear in mind that the large discretionary powers held by Immigration Authorities tend to mitigate the differences. On the other hand, Portuguese membership of the European Community is likely to lead to a process of unification of laws and procedures with the other Member States, thus causing significant changes in the legal system.

11.4   The government has continued to evidence a far more favourable approach to applications in cases of property investment or establishment of a business in Portugal. Due to this reason particular attention will be devoted in this chapter to aspects related to these categories as being the easiest way to obtain a Portuguese residence permit.

At the end of March 1992, the Portuguese government introduced a bill in the Parliament with the main purpose of legalising the situation of illegal foreigners in the country. This bill affects in particular nationals of Brazil and former African colonies, and basically stipulates that those foreigners may be allowed to remain in Portugal if they have entered the country prior to 1 June 1986. Another bill revising the legal regime of entrance, permanent residence and exit of foreign nationals is also presently being discussed in Parliament and if approved will introduce significant changes in these matters (see the Appendix at the end of this chapter).

[*The next paragraph is 11.8.*]

1. Permanent immigrants

(i) General procedure and requirements

11.8   Persons applying for residence under this category are normally required to submit their application for a residence visa with the Portuguese consulate of their place of residence. In some very particular cases non-EC nationals may apply directly for a residence permit with the Aliens Service Office (*Serviço de Estrangeiros*) in Portugal, if they are able to prove that they do not have fixed residence in another country. However, in the latter case they should always obtain an entry visa if they are not nationals of any of the countries referred to in paras 11.23–11.24.

Children under 14 years old are automatically included in their parents' application, while others over 14 and under 21 years old may not be required to submit a separate application if they are still living with their parents.

11.9   The Immigration Authorities normally follow criteria for evaluating the applications, considering the following conditions:
- fulfilment by the applicant(s) of Portuguese laws;
- reasons for requiring a resident visa and their pertinence;

- existence of family connections with Portuguese residents;
- financial capability (in this respect some consular offices might require copies of bank accounts, the opening of a bank account with a Portuguese Bank, or other evidence of the applicant's means of subsistence);
- investment in Portugal;
- adequate housing conditions in Portugal (for this purpose some consulates might demand a certificate obtained locally attesting the ownership of a house);
- health and criminal records.

After the residence visa is granted foreigners from non-EC Member **11.10** States should travel to Portugal in the next four months to apply for a residence permit with the Aliens Service Office. Some additional documents must then be produced to the said authority depending on the category of the application. However, common experience shows that if the residence visa was granted, the issue of the residence permit is usually a mere formality.

The residence permit is normally valid for a period of one year, and is renewable without major difficulties every year. Nevertheless, the Immigration Authorities may in certain cases deny the renewal of the residence permit if the foreign citizen has spent most of the time out of the country. The foreign resident is obliged to communicate to the Immigration Authorities if he intends to reside outside Portugal for more than 90 days. After legally residing in the country for five years a foreign resident may apply for a residence card renewable every five years, and following 20 years of residence, a card valid for 20 years may be applied for.

After obtaining their residence permit, non-EC nationals should register **11.11** with their country's consular office.

In addition to the procedures and formalities described above, other documents should be produced together with the general ones as per the following social and economic groups.

(ii) **Employees of a private individual, company or organisation**

When applying for a residence visa, persons under this category should deliver **11.12** to the Portuguese consulate of their country of origin or residence, a written advice from their future employer clearly showing that they have been offered employment, together with a formal document of approval issued by the Ministry of Labour. When applying for a residence permit in Portugal, they should deliver a copy of their contract of work.

(iii) **Self-employed persons/liberal professionals**

Foreign citizens in these conditions shall prove, when applying for a residence **11.13** visa, that they hold the necessary qualifications to exercise their profession within the Portuguese legal framework. In case of some Liberal Professionals

(Lawyers, doctors, etc) a previous authorisation from their respective Bar or professional association is also required.

(iv) Business

11.14   One of the most frequent methods used to obtain residence in Portugal is through this category, therefore justifying a brief explanation on the basic procedures required to invest in the country.

    Since accession to the European Community, Portuguese legislation on foreign investment has been significantly liberalised. Apart from some sectors, such as defence industries and some public services, the new legislation on foreign investment guarantees the right of establishment, take over or joint-venture in all sectors open to private enterprise with no discrimination based on the investors' nationality. Also there are no restrictions on the percentage of foreign ownership allowed and it is possible to form a company entirely owned by non-resident investors.

11.15   Investment authorisations are granted by ICEP (The Foreign Trade Institute), which will not generally disallow investments originating from outside the European Community provided they comply with certain minimum legal requirements. Foreign investors are subject to a requirement to lodge with ICEP a declaration of intent to invest, giving details of the operation and submitting the necessary documentation.

    All persons applying under this category should produce to the Portuguese consulate the declaration approved by ICEP relevant to the enterprise they wish to establish/purchase/join. In principle, there is no minimum amount to be invested and the foreign investor may freely decide the allocation of funds for investment purposes. However, the Immigration Authorities are more likely to grant a visa to foreign investors whose projects feature, amongst others, the following characteristics: a considerable financial investment; the utilisation of the investors' own money; the management and direction of the business by the same investors; and the creation of employment for Portuguese citizens.

11.16   The foreign investor should always produce documentary proof showing that a bank account in Portuguese escudos has been opened, issued by the bank concerned. The amount to be deposited may vary from case to case, and is defined by the Immigration Authorities.

(v) Property investment

11.17   Application for residence by means of property investment is undoubtedly the easiest way to obtain residence in Portugal. In spite of recent directives aimed to control the overwhelming number of applications under this category, it still remains the most popular and simple form of applying for residence in the country.

    Upon delivery of documents to the Portuguese consulate, foreign citizens are also obliged to produce a legalised copy of the Property's Promissory Contract of Purchase and Sale. However, consular offices located in certain countries have instructions to demand not merely the document proving a promise to purchase, but the notarial deed of Purchase and Sale, which means that in those countries the respective nationals will have to purchase the property prior to obtaining the visa for residence. In any case the property has to be completely free of charges or encumbrances and cannot be allocated for rent.

Property investors shall, likewise, show documentary proof that a bank **11.18** account in Portuguese escudos has been opened, issued by the Bank concerned. As explained in paras 11.14–11.16 the required amounts to be deposited may vary from case to case.

(vi) **Persons of independent means/investors**

Persons of independent means must produce some documentary proof to the **11.19** Portuguese consulate showing that a bank account in a Portuguese bank has been opened, issued by the bank concerned. The first deposit shall not be inferior to twelve times the minimum gross earnings index in the applicant's country of origin and per each member of the family. The aforementioned gross earnings index shall in no case be inferior to the minimum gross earnings index settled for the services sector in Portugal.

When applying in Portugal for the residence permit, these persons must produce a copy of their latest bank account statement.

(vii) **Pensioners/retired persons**

Pensioners or retired persons applying for residence in Portugal must produce **11.20** documentary proof of their retirement indicating their income. They are also required to open a bank account in Portuguese escudos, and the bank concerned must issue the corresponding certification.

In any case the monthly credit balance shall not be inferior to the minimum gross earnings index in the applicant's country of origin, per each member of the family.

(viii) **Ministers of religion, missionaries and members of religious orders**

These persons must deliver to the Portuguese consular office a statement from **11.21** the religious order or congregation indicating the area and the location where they will be based, together with documentary proof of the financial means their respective congregation has secured for their maintenance while in Portugal.

(ix) **Family reunion/joining relatives**

"Relatives" are defined as: ancestors or descendents of first degree, for **11.22** example children joining their parents and vice-versa. Applicants under these circumstances must produce documentary proof that they are related to the person they are going to join. The Immigration Authorities should also demand an official written proof of the relative's financial capability or a letter from the relative's employer confirming his appointment to be either on a temporary or permanent basis, detailing current salary. Finally a residence certificate of the relative established in Portugal is also needed for application purposes.

2. Visitors and students

(i) Visitors

11.23 Foreign citizens visiting Portugal for a temporary purpose (tourism, business, etc) may usually remain in Portugal for a period of two or three months without the necessity of a visa if they are nationals of Western European, North American and some South American countries (the same applies to citizens from Australia, New Zealand, Japan, South Korea, Malawi and Swaziland). People from other parts of the world must produce to Immigration Officers a tourist or business visa usually valid for a short period of time, and which is normally applied for with the Portuguese consulate of their country of origin.

11.24 Nationals of Austria, Switzerland, Malta and Turkey may enter the country for the purpose of visiting under the same conditions as EC nationals, *i.e.* without a passport as they may simply produce their valid national identity cards.

Holders of travel documents issued in Europe under the Geneva Convention of 28 July 1951 do not require visas to enter and sojourn in Portugal for a period of three months for purposes of tourism and commercial business.

(ii) Students

11.25 Foreign nationals wishing to enter Portugal as students must apply for a residence visa with the Portuguese consulate abroad before leaving their country. When applying for such a visa, and in addition to the general requirements outlined below in paras 11.8–11.11, they must produce a statement in which it is clearly shown that they are enrolled at a certain academic institution to attend a course. They will also be required to show some documentary proof of the financial means they have secured for their maintenance in Portugal. In the case of scholarship or bursary holders, applicants must deliver a declaration from the establishment where they are to further their studies, showing clearly the title of the body granting the scholarship or bursary and respective duration; this document should be authorised by the competent department of the Portuguese Ministry of

Foreign Affairs. After the visa for residence is granted, the foreign national must travel to Portugal to apply for a residence permit with the Aliens Service Office (*Serviço de Estrangeiros*).

3. Refugees and political asylum

The right of asylum may be granted to: (i) foreigners persecuted or **11.26** dangerously threatened with persecution in their country of origin as a result of activities in favour of democracy, freedom, peace or human rights; (ii) to foreigners who fear persecution on the grounds of race, religion, nationality, political opinions or integration in a certain social group; and (iii) to foreigners who are fleeing armed struggles or violation of human rights in their country of origin.

Right of asylum will automatically be denied to foreigners who have taken any acts against the fundamental interest and sovereignty of Portugal; who have committed war crimes, crimes against peace, or crimes against humankind, as they are defined in international conventions; and finally may be denied for reasons of national security.

The application for asylum should be filed with the Aliens Service Office. **11.27** Any foreigners illegally entering Portugal for the purpose of acquiring political asylum should file such request to the competent authority without further delay. The application for political asylum may include close relatives of the applicant, if the latter so wishes.

Applicants for political asylum who can prove that they lack the minimum financial capability to support themselves and their family may benefit from social security assistance until the Aliens Service Office has decided their request for asylum in Portugal.

Any person under the status of political asylum enjoys the same rights and is subject to the same duties as any other foreigner residing in Portugal.

4. Nationality

(i) Birth

Children born of Portuguese parents (father and/or mother) in Portuguese **11.28** territory, or abroad in case any of the parents is employed officially by the Portuguese state, are automatically considered as nationals of Portugal. Children born of Portuguese citizens while abroad and whose parents were not officially representing the Portuguese state, may upon reaching full age, choose Portuguese citizenship.

Children born in Portugal of foreign parents who have been residents in Portugal for a minimum of six years and who were not officially representing a foreign country, may also acquire Portuguese nationality, provided that upon reaching full age they declare it to be their intention.

(ii) **Marriage**

11.29 A foreign national married to a Portuguese citizen may choose to acquire Portuguese citizenship.

(iii) **Naturalisation**

11.30 In order to apply for Portuguese citizenship under this category, a certain number of conditions have to be fulfilled, including:
- full age (18 years old or over);
- legal residence in Portugal or Macau for at least six years;
- sufficient knowledge of the Portuguese language, the applicant being in certain cases required to take a test before a Portuguese official or, alternatively, to produce a legalised diploma issued by a Portuguese school;
- good character;
- good financial capability – the applicant has to prove that he is able to support himself and his family, and in some circumstances will have to produce documentary evidence of his means of subsistence.

Applicants who have Portuguese ancestors, are members of communities with Portuguese roots or have rendered relevant services to the Portuguese state, may be excused from proving both their residence in Portugal and their knowledge of the Portuguese language.

11.31 The decision to grant citizenship is taken by the Ministry of Internal Affairs, which holds considerable discretionary power in these matters. Naturalisation may be denied, among other reasons, if: (i) there is not an effective connection with Portugal; (ii) if the foreign citizen was convicted for a serious crime in another country; or (iii) if the applicant was previously a public official of a foreign state or was enlisted in its armed forces.

5. **Sanctions**

Eviction

11.32 Without prejudice to international treaties signed by Portugal and which foresee cases for eviction, the grounds for eviction of foreign citizens according to Portuguese law are the following: (i) irregular entrance into Portugal; (ii) menace to national security and public order; (iii) interference by any means with Portuguese public officials; (iv) disregard of Portuguese laws and regulations applicable to foreigners; and (v) conviction of a certain type of crime.

The Aliens Service Office is charged with organising the files, collecting the necessary evidence and documentation and afterwards filing the eviction procedure with the court. The judge upon receipt of such file should schedule the judgment for the next 48 hours, assuring that the foreigner has adequate means of defence. The court's sentence should imperatively indicate: the delay period for its enforcement (a maximum of 40 days for residents and 8 days for non-residents); the period during which the foreigner shall be forbidden to return to Portugal; and the foreigner's country of destination.

The court sentence deciding the eviction may be subject to an appeal to a Higher Court, *but such appeal does not have suspensive effect.*

The foreign citizen cannot be evicted to a country where he may be persecuted for political reasons.

11.33

Appendix – Legislation

A11.1 The more relevant laws presently in force are:
- Decree Law 246-C/81 of 3 September 1981 (Entry, Permanence and Exit of non-EC citizens)
- Decree Law 267/87 of 2 July 1987 (Entry, Permanence and Exit of EC citizens)
- Decree Law 97/77 of 17 March 1977 (Foreigners working in Portugal)

A11.2 The Portuguese government introduced in April 1992 a bill in Parliament which is still under discussion, and if approved will introduce significant changes in the legal régime of entrance, permanence and exit of Foreign Nationals. The purposes of such a bill are amongst others to:
- implement the applicable EC Directives and clarify the entry and permanence of EC citizens;
- clarify the criteria and procedures for the obtention of visas and residence permits;
- facilitate the process of eviction, enlarging the powers of judicial authorities, and foreseeing the possibility in certain cases of administrative authorities to decide in these matters;
- introduce the crime of "Violation of Eviction Order", punishable with a prison term of up to two years or a pecuniary penalty;
- create the crime of "Assistance to Illegal Immigration", with penalty terms of up to five years; and
- adapt the legal system of infractions to illegal permanence, lack of working and/or residence permit, unlawful use of travel documents and disregard of the resident's obligations.

Spain

Chapter 12
Spain

1. Permanent immigrants

(i) Employment

(a) Work permits

All foreigners who would like to work in Spain as employees need to obtain a **12.1** work permit (*permiso de trabajo*) granted by the Spanish authorities. However, if exceptional circumstances concur, the Ministry of Labour and Social Security may recognise some other documents as having the same effect as a work permit. In order to obtain a work permit, the applicant must produce a written labour contract, or if this is not possible, at least a formal promise of employment from an employer who is expecting the foreign person to render labour services under this direction.

There are three types of work permit in Spain: **12.2**

Type A: this work permit is valid for a period of nine months, and cannot be renewed. It allows its holder to practice only temporary or cyclic activities, and the worker must leave Spain no longer than fifteen days after its expiry date.

Type B: this kind of permit is issued for a maximum period of one year and allows the holder to work in a specified profession, activity and geographical zone. This permit can be renewed, but only for one more year. However, the authorities may exceptionally extend the effects of the permit, if the employee is obtaining benefits as consequence of a labour accident or sickness.

Type C: this permit consists of an administrative authorisation for the holder to work in any kind of activity anywhere on Spanish territory for a maximum period of five years.

Applications for obtaining work permits must usually be made by the **12.3** employer who wishes the foreign person to work for them. There is only one exception: work permit Type C. In this case it is the worker himself who must apply to obtain authorisation. Applications must always be made before the beginning of the labour relationship, excluding permit renewals; in these cases the employer must apply for an extension of at least one month before the expiry date of the permit (in those cases in which it is possible). There are official documents prepared by the administration which must be used to make applications.

There are certain circumstances under which the Labour Authorities may **12.4** refuse an application for work permits Type A and B. Among them are:

159

(i)   when there is high unemployment in Spain;

(ii)   when the labour conditions stated in the contract (which must be included on the application) are below the standard established by Spanish labour laws;

(iii) when the application has been made by a foreign employer who is not legally established in Spain;

(iv) when the employer who makes the application defaults on the obligations set by Spanish legislation;

(v)   when there are false or inaccurate statements on the application or when it is accompanied by false documents; or

(vi) when the Labour Authorities consider that there are sufficient grounds for refusing to grant the permit. This last reason for refusing to grant a permit is at the discretion of the Spanish Authorities. However, refusal must be reasonably justified, and in any case, resolutions of this kind must always (if considered to be against the law, equity, or are taken on discretionary grounds under which other foreigners in similar circumstances were granted a permit) be submitted to the judicial authorities to guarantee the legitimacy of the resolution.

12.5   Work permit Type C, can only be issued under the following circumstances:

(i)   if the foreign worker has been the holder of other types of work permits issued for a period of no longer than five years; or

(ii)   if the worker has been legally resident in Spain for a period of eight years and has been the holder of other types of work permits in the twelve months previous to the application for work permit Type C.

(b) Preference given for obtaining work permits

12.6   In order to obtain work permits there are certain foreigners who may be preferred on the basis of different circumstances and depending upon the type of permit they wish to obtain.

Regarding permits A and B, conditions for preference in obtaining the authorisation are based mainly on family considerations. Spanish legislation gives priority to those workers who are married to a Spanish national, who are in charge of descendants or ascendants of Spanish nationals, or who are closely related (first grade) to the employer. There are also other circumstances which can be taken into consideration for preference in obtaining these permits, for example preference for asylum seekers or refugees.

12.7   Priority or preference regarding work permit Type C is also given to those foreigners born in countries closely connected to Spain by historical circumstances. These include: nationals from South and Central America, Portugal, the Philippines or Ecuatorial Guinea. Priority is also given to those applications made by foreigners who are descendants of foreigners who once had Spanish nationality, and are resident in Spain when making their application.

(c) Exceptions

12.8   Spanish laws contemplate certain exceptions to the general regime of work permits, which can be analysed on the basis of three different grounds.

(i) Exceptions based on international relations between different countries in the international community. They include diplomatic and consular functionaries (as well as their families) of permanent missions, or members of delegations of international organisations located in Spain. The exception also includes functionaries working in inter-government-al organisations located in Spain.

(ii) Exceptions based on the development of culture and science. This category exempts from obtaining work permits, in order to make it easier for them to work in Spain for the development of culture and science, all those foreign technicians and scientists who have entered into a contract with the Spanish state, as well as professors invited by a Spanish university. Also included are members of international scient-ific missions carrying out research in Spain (in this case they must obtain an authorisation from the authorities to carry out their research before entering Spain).

(iii) Exceptions based on specific professions and activities. These include:
   - journalists representing newspapers or agencies as well as general broadcasting organisations (however, they must be bearers of accreditation, obtained legally, which enable them to carry out their reporting activities);
   - priests and nuns, and representatives of religious missions, but only if they limit their activity strictly to religious works (this exception extends only to those religions which are legally registered in Spain);
   - artists, when acting continuously in Spain.

(ii) Business

People who would like to develop a business in Spain, working by their own means, must also obtain a work permit. The legal system regarding business is also based on the system of work permits. This system provides a transitory status under work permit Type D, which enables its holder to develop a business only in a certain geographical area and for a period of time no longer than one year. In order to obtain this permit, the applicant must be able to demonstrate the he has already obtained from the Spanish Authorities all the authorisations that would be necessary for nationals to open and run the same activity.   **12.9**

After this transitory period, foreign businessmen must be able to demon-strate, if they want to continue with their activity that: **12.10**
   - they are already legally established;
   - they have fulfilled all their obligations regarding taxes and Social Security;
   - they are dedicated full-time to that activity.

After having well fulfilled these conditions, they may obtain the work permit Type E, provided they obtain favourable references from:
   - the local Directorate of Economy and Trade;
   - the Official Chamber of Trade, Industry and Navigation or of the Chamber of Agriculture; and
   - the corresponding services of the council.

12.11   All these references taken together will provide the points of view of territorial and local administrations as well as those of representative chambers as to the kind of activity and the way it is carried out. The Authorities will then have an informed basis upon which they may decide whether to grant the work permit or not.

(iii) **Family and marriage**

12.12   All those foreign individuals who may have the intention of living permanently (resident) in Spain must obtain a "residence visa" (*visado de residencia*). This visa can be obtained for family reasons by the following:
(i)   spouses of Spanish nationals or of foreigners legally resident in Spain;
(ii)   children under 18;
(iii)   children over 18 when dependent legally and economically on Spanish nationals or foreigners resident in Spain;
(iv)   disabled children under 18 whose legal representatives may be Spanish nationals or foreigners legally resident in Spain;
(v)   foreign descendants or ascendants of Spanish nationals or of other foreigners resident in Spain.

12.13   In order to obtain the visa it is necessary to prove the relationship and in certain cases the economic dependence.

Family and marriage are also decisive factors for obtaining a residence permit. This kind of permit can be granted to those foreigners who have no intention of establishing or working in Spain. Spanish laws contemplate special permits of this kind for:
– foreigners married to nationals with residence in Spain;
– foreigners legally in charge of ascendants or descendants with Spanish nationality.

12.14   Children born in Spain whose parents do not have Spanish nationality, are considered to be nationals in origin in two cases. First, when their parents lack any nationality or if the law applying to them does not recognise their nationality to their children who were born outside their homeland. The main reason for granting the Spanish nationality to these children is to avoid the problem of stateless people. Spanish law makes use of the *ius loci* and adopts as nationals those children who otherwise would lack a nationality. The second case applies to those children born in Spain of foreign parents where, at least, one of them also was also born in Spain. In this case the law is trying to avoid the continuous perpetuation of foreign families established and resident in Spain. Legally the second generation of these foreign families will bear Spanish nationality.

12.15   There are certain special rules for those whose family links or place of birth are determined when they are over 18 years of age (Spanish legal majority age). In these cases, the granting of Spanish nationality is not automatic but conditional upon the decision of the interested person who may choose to bear Spanish nationality. The choice has to be made within the two years following the determination of the family link or place of birth.

In the case of adoption, when foreigners under 18 are adopted by Spanish **12.16**
nationals they automatically become holders of Spanish nationality. If the
adoption is completed after the adopted person reaches full age (*i.e.* 18 years),
the adopted foreigner must decide himself whether to bear Spanish nationality
within the two years following the adoption.

2. **Visitors, students and temporary workers**

All those nationals of foreign countries who wish to enter into Spanish territory **12.17**
must have one of the following documents in order to prove their identity:
(i)   passport, legally issued, either personal or collective;
(ii)   travel documents; and
(iii)   identity documents or other documents provided for in international
        treaties.
A visa is also necessary, except for those nationals who intend to stay for no
longer than 90 days and who originate from a country exempted from this
condition.

The entrance and exit to and from Spain must necessarily be made through **12.18**
the special points set out by the authorities, and under control of functionaries
of the Ministry of Interior. Functionaries in charge of these points may ask
foreigners to demonstrate sufficient means of support for the period of their
stay in Spain and for their return journey to their home country or to another
country. In exceptional circumstances the Ministry of Interior and the
Ministry of Health may ask for medical certificates from those intending to
enter into Spain. These certificates, from medical services designated by the
Spanish embassy at the country of origin of the foreigner, must demonstrate
that the holder does not suffer from any contagious diseases which are
dangerous to public health, drug addiction or mental illness which may
threaten Spanish safety or public order. If they do not have such a certificate,
foreigners must undergo a medical check at the frontier to be carried out by the
medical services established by the Spanish authorities.

(i) **Foreigners in transit**

Holders of passports or any other valid document for entrance to Spain, **12.19**
with a visa issued for a period of no longer than 30 days, will only be allowed to
remain in Spain for the period of time necessary to achieve the objective of
their journey.

When extraordinary circumstances make it impossible for them to leave
Spain within the period of time specified in the authorisation, Civil Governors
or the General Directorate of Police may extend the authorisation for the
required period.

163

(ii) **Tourist visits or similar**

12.20   Foreigners coming to Spain for tourism or leisure, to practice non-professional sports, to make a pilgrimage or to undertake brief studies or courses may remain in Spain, if they are not involved in any professional activity, for three months or for the period of time which is stated on the visa (when necessary) or has otherwise been authorised.

They must leave Spain before the expiry of their authorisation, or apply for an extension of up to a further three months. This application must be made at least 15 days before expiry of the previous authorised period. If the foreigner wishes to remain for a longer period of time, he must then apply for a residence permit.

(iii) **Foreign students**

12.21   Foreign students entering Spain are subject to a special regime. Those who want to carry out long-term studies in Spain must submit an application to the Diplomatic representatives of Spain in their country of residence who can issue a visa. Once they have obtained this visa, students may then obtain a student's card from the Ministry of Interior. This card enables students to remain in Spain provided they:

(i)   Have fulfilled all the requirements necessary for their entrance and stay in Spain, which are the same as for any other foreign person who may wish to enter Spain.

(ii)   Have already been admitted as pupils, students or researchers in either public or otherwise authorised centres for a period of time under three months and following weekly time-tables over 15 hours of study. The special conditions applying to students can only be made effective if the interested student is already admitted as such in an authorised centre. This will guarantee that those intending to enter Spain as students are in fact going to dedicate their time to study.

(iii)   Have enough means to support not only the cost of their studies, but also their upkeep while studying and their journey back to their home country.

3. **Refugees and political asylum**

12.22   Following the principles set out by the Spanish constitution, Spanish law tries to give an effective answer to the problem of refugees who are unable to live freely in their countries of origin because of ideological or political reasons. Spain tries to treat these refugees according to certain principles such as solidarity, hospitality and tolerance.

The right of asylum has undergone a serious transformation (and not only in Spain). Originally it provided a way of protecting common criminals. Now it has become a procedure for protecting only those pursued for political reasons (including, in a broad sense, persecution connected with colour, religion, nationality etc).

The Spanish system of political asylum affords two different kinds of protection: **12.23**

(i) The first level (primary protection) consists of disregarding extradition applications so that the beneficiary of asylum is not forced to return to his country of origin. Thus, whenever a foreign individual entering Spain applies for asylum, that individual may not be extradited until the authorities resolve whether to grant or deny asylum.

(ii) A second level of protection includes certain benefits for the asylum seeker to make his future life in Spain easier. These benefits include:
   – authorisations to reside in Spain;
   – issuing of ID and travel documentation;
   – authorisations to perform labour and professional activities; and
   – other benefits contemplated in international conventions.

As far as political asylum is concerned it should be mentioned that applications can be made at the Spanish border (frontier) or even inside Spanish territory. Asylum, when granted, extends to the spouse and first degree descendants. **12.24**

Benefit of asylum may only be granted by the government itself through an inter-ministry commission (formed by ministers of those departments directly connected with political asylum affairs).

Spain will grant refugee status to all those people that fulfil the requirements set out by the laws and international treaties to which it is a party, and especially the Geneva Convention of 1951.

4. Nationality

Legal residence in Spain, for a certain period of time, may lead to gaining Spanish nationality (at the interested person's choice). The period of time may be different according to different circumstances. These can be distinguished as follows: **12.25**

(i) 10 years of legal residence; this could be called the general rule. Any foreigner coming legally to Spain and remaining as resident for 10 years may obtain Spanish nationality.

(ii) The period of time applicable to refugees and asylum seekers is five years. This reduction by half of the time usually applied is part of the benefits granted to asylum seekers and refugees.

(iii) For those nationals of South American countries, the Philippines, Andorra, Ecuatorial Guinea, Portugal and Jewish communities the period is two years. The main reason for this shorter period of time is the historic links that join Spain with these foreign countries and communities.

(iv)　Only one year of legal residence is required for family reasons or territory. In this group can be included: those people who, at the time of their application, have been married for at least one year to a Spanish person; or the widow of a Spanish person (providing that at the time of the death of the spouse there was no divorce or legal or factual separation).

12.26　　When applying for Spanish nationality by means of residence, the foreigner must justify his good civic conduct and enough integration into the Spanish way of life.

The granting of Spanish nationality will, finally, be conditional upon the fulfilment of the following:

(i)　swear or promise of fidelity to the King and obedience to the Spanish Constitution and laws;

(ii)　waiving the right to previous nationality (except in certain cases); and

(iii)　registration of Spanish nationality in the Civil Registry.

5. Sanctions

(i) Deportation

12.27　　Foreigners in one of the following situations are liable to deportation:

(i)　illegal stay in Spanish territory without a residence permit;

(ii)　working without the necessary work permit, although holding a valid residence permit;

(iii)　being involved in certain activities contrary to public order or to the safety of the state, or activities against the international interest of Spain, or which may cause damage to the international relations between Spain and other countries;

(iv)　having been convicted, inside or outside Spain, of an offence considered in Spain to be a crime which would be ordinarily punished by imprisonment for a period longer than one year; or

(v)　having no legal economic means to live, living on alms or begging or living on illegal means.

(ii) Economic sanctions

12.28　　Transgression of Spanish laws regarding immigration in relation to the entrance, situation and exit of foreigners may also in some cases be subject to economic sanctions.

(iii) Sanctions for employers

12.29　　Not only the foreigners, but also employers who use illegal immigrants for labour can be sanctioned. Those employers who give work to foreigners who are not holders of a work permit will be sanctioned according to the labour laws. Employers will be fined for each of the foreigners that they have illegally employed. This is considered to be a major breach of the rules according to labour laws.

6. **Social security considerations**

Regarding social security, once again Spanish laws take into account the links **12.30** that once existed historically between Spain and other nations, in order to distinguish between two different social security systems. All those foreign workers who come to Spain from Latin America, Portugal, Brazil, Andorra or The Philippines, if legally established in Spain are considered to have equal rights to Spanish nationals with respect to social security.

For all other foreign workers, the social security system applying to them will be either one resulting from international treaties to which Spain is a party or from the general principle of reciprocity, *i.e.* foreign workers in Spain be accorded the same social security system as that applied to Spanish workers in the foreign workers' country of origin.

Sweden

Chapter 13
Sweden

Unlike all the other countries covered in this book, Sweden is not yet a member **13.1**
of the European Community. However, the EC Council meeting in Edin-
burgh in December 1992 resulted in a favourable view that Sweden would
become a full member by 1995. Of the two other Scandinavian states,
Denmark and Norway, Denmark has been a member of the European
Community for some time and Norway filed its application for membership in
1992.

Sweden is a member of the European Free Trade Association (EFTA). In **13.2**
November 1991 EFTA signed a treaty with the European Community which
would have meant free access from 1 January 1993 for EC and EFTA nationals
to each others territories. The treaty would have had enormous influence upon
the free movement of people from participating states and – in some instances –
of third country nationals. However, the Swiss rejected the treaty in a
referendum on 6 December 1992 and the start date of the treaty has now been
delayed for up to a year.

If the EC/EFTA treaty comes into force in late 1993, free movement rights **13.3**
will apply immediately to EFTA and EC nationals in 19 states. However,
there will probably be transitional periods in Switzerland and Liechtenstein.
Only those with an offer of employment will be able to take advantage of the
situation; those who do not will have the right to stay in Sweden for three
months while they look for one.

Introduction

Sweden has a total area of 450,000 square kilometres and a population on 31 **13.4**
December 1991 of 8,644,119 of which 493,848 are aliens. The total value of
imports and exports in 1990 was 662,626 MSEK with exports of 25.4% of
GDP. Sweden's main trading partners are Germany, the United Kingdom,
the United States and the other Nordic countries, with 14%, 10%, 9% and
22% respectively of total exports. The average hourly wage for adult earners
in 1991 was 76 SEK (Swedish Crowns = "kroner") for men and 67 SEK for
women.

The number of inhabitants per square kilometre in the Netherlands is 362, **13.5**
in Germany 249, in France 102 and in Sweden only 19. There has been a
certain amount of immigration to Sweden during many different periods of
history. From the 1930s immigrants have outnumbered emigrants, and since

then net migration has accounted for a progressively larger share of total population growth. From the early 1970s, net migration to and from Sweden accounted for 70–80% of population growth. Sweden today is a country of greater ethnic diversity than ever before. Nearly 10% of Sweden's population are immigrants or have immigrant parents.

1. Permanent immigrants

(i) Immigrants not performing professional activities

(a) Persons of independent means

13.6 Non-working persons, such as those of independent means, cannot expect to obtain a residence permit in Sweden. Fifty years of socialism in Sweden hinder aliens from being able to "buy" a place in Swedish society.

(b) Family reunion

13.7 Relatives of an immigrant who has become a Swedish citizen or who lives in Sweden with a residence permit (PUT) will be able to reunite with their relative in Sweden under the following circumstances:

(i)   An application from a husband/wife or minor of a Swedish citizen or foreign citizen legally settled in Sweden cannot be denied. The Immigration Board usually demands two years of cohabitation abroad or that the spouses have a child together. Cohabitation outside marriage is treated in the same way and children under 20 who are not married are also accepted.

(ii)   If cohabitation has been for less than two years, then a residence permit can be granted for a renewable six-month period, with a police investigation after each period.

(iii)   Marriages where one of the partners is under 18 or which are polygamous are discriminated against and permits are never granted.

(iv)   Foreign, unmarried children under the age of 16 do not require a residence permit if the parent in whose custody they reside is a citizen of Sweden, Denmark, Finland, Iceland or Norway, or is settled in Sweden with a valid residence permit. Children between the ages of 16 and 20 can be denied a permit if they have not regularly resided with the parent in Sweden from an early age.

(v)   A parent of an immigrant who has become a widow/widower and has a child under 16 will normally be given a residence permit if the majority of his children live in Sweden.

(vi)   A single parent who is at least 60 years old without accompanying children is normally given a permit to settle with children domiciled in Sweden. The number of children in his country of residence or in Sweden is of no importance. However, if it is clear that the parent intends to live on maintenance from the Swedish social welfare the application for a residence permit will be denied.

(vii)   Reunion with both parents, if they are at least 60 years old, is allowed if all their children are domiciled in Sweden or there are strong humanitarian grounds.

(viii)   The last member of a nuclear family can be given a residence permit.

(c) Residence permit (*Uppehållstillstånd (UT)*)

All immigrants who are not Nordic citizens have to obtain the necessary permits before arrival in Sweden. (This, of course, does not apply to convention refugees.)   **13.8**

Aliens with a passport can enter Sweden and stay for three months without a special permit. Usually no questions are asked at border control and no forms have to be filled in. A foreigner without visible means of support or a return ticket may be denied entry. Citizens from some countries have to have a visa before entering Sweden.

A person over the age of 16 who wishes to stay in Sweden for more than three months has to obtain a residence permit and have sufficient means of living.

A person under the age of 16 does not require a residence permit if his custodian lives in Sweden or has a residence permit. A residence permit is usually issued for a certain period or as a permanent residence permit.   **13.9**

A residence permit which is valid for a limited period is usually given to guest students, practitioners, scientists and researchers and persons who wish to stay in Sweden for longer than three months.

(d) Permanent residence permit (*Permanent Uppehållstillstånd (PUT)*)

PUT grants permission to stay in Sweden for an unlimited period. It can be applied for by a person who has had: **13.10**
(i)   a work permit for more than one year;
(ii)   a residence permit for more than one year and is married to a Swedish citizen, or an alien with an alien's passport (Främlingspass) and who does not require a work permit;
(iii)   a residence permit for more than one year and who, after application, would be granted a work permit if one was applied for (*e.g.* a person who is married to a holder of a residence and work permit).

A permanent residence permit expires when the alien becomes a Swedish citizen. When a holder of a permanent residence permit finally renounces residence in Sweden, the permit then expires.

(ii) Immigrants performing professional activities

(a) Employees

Citizens of Nordic countries do not require a work permit to work in Sweden. However, aliens from other states should apply for a work permit before entry. Only if they arrive in Sweden to reunite with a member of their family with a residence permit, can a work permit be granted after entry.   **13.11**

173

A work permit is not needed by an alien who:
(i)   has a permanent residence permit (usually given after one year);
(ii)   is married to a Swedish citizen; or
(iii)   who has not reached the age of 16, if their custodian has a residence permit.

13.12   Foreign workers with special skills will have no problems obtaining a work permit if they are to be employed as researchers by Swedish companies or scientific institutions.

Foreigners working on Swedish ships abroad do not require work permits, provided the shipping company has been given a permit to employ the alien in question.

13.13   Work permits are not required for one month of artistic work for the Swedish Broadcasting Corporation, nor for the first two months after entry for mechanics or technical instructors, nor for the first three months after entry for foreign drivers of foreign trucks and tourist buses, nurses accompanying persons visiting Sweden for medical care or recreation, scientists who have been asked to lecture or teach at a Swedish university or for guest students for the period 15 May–15 September.

Before a work permit is issued, a labour market investigation is carried out by the National Labour Market Board and the National Immigration Board following recommendations from trade unions and the labour authorities. A work permit is usually granted for one year. Exceptions are rarely applied.

(b) Self-employed persons, traders, merchants and businessmen

13.14   Sweden does not yet acknowledge a right for an alien to "buy" a place in Swedish society through investment. The amount of interest for investing in business opportunities in Sweden is still low. However, after nearly 50 years of socialism the new government elected on 15 September 1991 is rapidly changing the laws in this respect.

At the present time, an alien wishing to move to Sweden to start a business has to obtain a residence permit and, almost always, a business permit as well. The application for a residence permit must be made through the Swedish embassy or consulate in the country of origin or residence. The application must contain:
(i)   information documenting access to the capital necessary to establish or purchase a company, and demonstrating sufficient means of support for at least one year in Sweden;
(ii)   a detailed business plan and full particulars of anything else which could be of importance, such as names of referees, bankers, business experience and prospects of success etc.

13.15   The embassy or consulate will then forward the application to the Swedish Immigration Board which will then make a decision. This could take up to three months. Notice of the Board's decision will be sent to the embassy or consulate where the application was submitted.

13.16   The residence permit must have been awarded and entered into the alien's passport before he enters Sweden. Residence permits are usually awarded for six-month periods for the first two years. Applications for extensions should be made to the local police. On the first occasion such an application is made, the police will check whether the alien has been able to support himself, whether he has been granted or applied for a business permit where necessary, and whether the business envisaged has been started. On subsequent occasions, the police will check that the alien is self-sufficient and that the business is being run as planned and that the alien has all the permits necessary to run such a business.

2. Visitors

(i) Visitors not performing professional activities

(a) Tourists (including family and business visitors)

Those possessing a valid passport can stay in Sweden as tourists for three **13.17** months provided sufficient means of maintenance is shown on entry. Those nationals of countries requiring a visa to enter Sweden should make their application to the Swedish embassy or consulate in their country of residence before starting their journey. A visa will not be issued at the Swedish border. Sweden does not have different types of business or other visas, but has different kinds of residence permits.

A negative decision given by the Immigration Board on a visa, work permit **13.18** or residence permit application cannot be appealed, but can be retried immediately if there are new circumstances. An application to retry should be given to the consulate or embassy in the country concerned, but if the foreigner is already in Sweden on a tourist visa, an application to prolong the visa can be filed at the local Police Board.

(b) Students

The criteria for admission are as follows: **13.19**

(i)   Guest students must have reached the age of 18 years and have had at least 11 years of education. They must have been admitted to a university before their application to the Swedish consulate or embassy in their country of residence seeking admission to Sweden.

(ii)   The applicant must show sufficient means of support for the whole length of the period of study. The amount necessary can vary from time to time. The study plan must be fixed and realistic. Proof of competence must also be supplied by an institution in the applicant's country of residence.

(iii)   The applicant is asked to sign a declaration that he will return to his home country once he has completed his studies. Guest students are not granted any social benefits, but are permitted to work for the period from 15 May to 15 September each year without a work permit.

(iv)   During the stay, sufficient evidence of the results of the studies has to be demonstrated according to the study plan each year. Swedish language education is arranged by the university.

(ii) **Visitors performing professional activities**

(a) Assigned employees and temporary workers

13.20 For some years now Sweden has observed a very restrictive policy as regards immigration of labour. In 1991 only about 3,000 citizens of unacknowledged countries were granted permanent residence permits for labour market reasons. Many more were granted residence and work permits for a limited period in order to carry out special assignments.

People from the business community will usually not encounter any problems when applying for a "business" visa to enter Sweden. The Swedish Immigration Board will issue a questionnaire to the Swedish company involved and will, after the receipt of the answer, grant a visa for one to three months, which can be extended.

13.21 A bi-lateral agreement between Sweden and the United States of 13 February 1992 established reciprocity between the two countries for issuing non-immigrant investor and trader visas.

It is extremely difficult to obtain a work permit as a means of settling in Sweden. There is a great deal of competition for job opportunities and Swedish and foreign nationals already living in Sweden have priority over persons living abroad and wishing to enter Sweden to settle.

13.22 When applying for a work permit the following procedure should be followed:

(i)   a valid passport is required together with a written offer of employment from the prospective employer in Sweden. This offer has to be made using a special form (AMS PF 1704) which the employer in Sweden can order from the Employment Service. The offer must show, *inter alia*, that the wages and other benefits will comply with current collective agreements. Secure housing arrangements must also be stipulated.

(ii)   Work permits have to be applied for through the Swedish embassy or consulate in the country of residence or domicile. The embassy/consulate has special application forms for this purpose.

(iii) The application will be forwarded by the embassy/consulate to the Swedish Immigration Board in Sweden, which will decide the matter in consultation with the labour board of the county where the prospective employment will be based.

(iv)   Notice of the decision will be sent to the embassy/consulate where the application was made. The procedure can take up to two months.

(v)   Before a work permit is issued, a labour market investigation is made by the National Labour Market Board and the National Immigration Board following recommendations made by the trade unions and the labour authorities. The work permit is usually granted for one year.

(vi)   The applicant may not enter Sweden until the work permit has been granted.

(c) Trainees

13.23 Trainees who wish to enter the country as temporary immigrants, who intend to work for a Swedish or foreign company and who can prove that the offer of training is satisfactory, should have no problems obtaining a short permit. It is presumed that the company can prove that the trainee has sufficient means of support and intends to return abroad after completion of the training. No ordinary employment can be permitted after the training period.

3. Refugees and political asylum

Investigations concerning asylum are made by special branches of the Local Police Authorities. It is possible for the refugee to obtain free legal aid from an advocate when the application comes before the Swedish Immigration Board. In the case of a negative decision, it is possible to appeal to the Aliens Board. Deportations are carried out by the police and staff from the National Prisons and Probation Administration.   **13.24**

On 15 June 1990 an EC Ministers' meeting in Dublin adopted a new convention on asylum legislation. This establishes, *inter alia*, which European country should be responsible for the investigation of an asylum case. Refugees will not be allowed to travel from one country to another to apply for asylum and will only be given one chance to apply for asylum within the European Community. In the case of a negative decision, no other nation within the Community will have an obligation to deal with the case again.   **13.25**

Five EC Member States signed the Schengen Agreement on 19 June 1990. This will mean that refugees from torture, war and bad conditions could, in future, meet closed borders when applying for asylum in Europe. The concept of "Fortress Europe" has been founded.

Sweden has adopted the established rule of "first country asylum", which entitles the police and Immigration Board to return an applicant for asylum to the country where he may have stopped on his journey to Sweden if that country is a signatory of the Geneva Convention and which does not intend to repatriate the refugee. A normal transfer through a country is normally not considered to be a "stop", but the Schengen Agreement will adversely affect the concept for the refugee. It remains to be seen what is considered "normal"; harmonisation of rights of asylum and procedures is still a long way away – a two-hour stop in Germany can correspond to a two-day stop in The Netherlands.   **13.26**

Before 1 July 1989 the following concept was used in Sweden: "Persecution is defined as persecution directed against the life or liberty of an alien or otherwise of a severe nature (political persecution)." Asylum in Sweden was also available to conscientious objectors and those known as "Class B" refugees, or could be granted on humanitarian grounds: "A residence permit could be granted if it is otherwise justifiable on humanitarian grounds." A Class B refugee was an alien who "although not a refugee, was unwilling to return to his home country on account of the political situation there, and was able to plead very strong grounds in support of his reluctance."   **13.27**

Most political refugees in Sweden are in fact Class B refugees. The meaning of "humanitarian grounds" was rather uncertain, but consideration was taken   **13.28** of severe illness or risk of suicide when a final deportation order was to be carried out.

On 31 May 1989 it was decided that families with children under the age of 16, who before that date had asked for asylum in Sweden and after the application had stayed in Sweden for more than one year, should be granted a permanent residence permit. Thus the concept of asylum-lottery was founded.

13.29   It was decided on 1 October 1989 that everyone who had sought asylum before 1 January 1989 should be granted a permanent residence permit, whatever the reasons they had stated. This was as a result of a backlog of applicants who had been waiting for some time and an inability by the authorities to decide their cases. It was confirmation of the asylum-lottery and it is easy to understand the despair felt by those who were borderline cases. During the autumn of 1989, for example, some 5,000 Bulgarian Turks claimed the right of asylum in Sweden.

On 14 December 1989 it was decided that the provision in the new Aliens Act concerning refugees (Chap 3, s 4, p 2) was to be interpreted in a new way. The old concept of classification of refugees as either Class A or B was to be abolished retroactively from 1 July 1989. A refugee in Sweden would now only be accepted if he (i) fulfils the requirements of the United Nations Convention on Refugees, or (ii) is in extraordinarily strong need of protection.

13.30   A stream of refugees followed from liberated countries, such as Romania. At the same time, countries like Poland and East Germany were considered as having acquired democratic status which meant that refugees coming from and through these countries were sent back. This new and unexpected situation had led to the new restrictions and in a press release dated 14 December 1989 the Swedish Ministry of Labour (including the office of the Minister of Immigration) stated that an increase of asylum seekers from 20,000 in 1988 to 30,000 in 1989 had necessitated the new harsher interpretation of the new law.

13.31   It is easy to understand that the criteria for determining refugee status under the 1951 Convention and the 1967 Geneva Protocol relating to the status of refugees were severely violated in Sweden. The government claimed that these instruments were not adapted to the reality of today.

On 1 January 1992 the new government abolished the restriction which has sent new signals to refugee producing countries. Up to 1 September 1992 Sweden had received 55,000 war refugees from the former Yugoslavia. Many experts argue that these refugees are so-called *de facto* refugees.

4. Nationality

13.32   Some 500,000 aliens were naturalised between 1948 and 1992. The tendency to apply for naturalisation varies depending upon the immigrant's country of origin and the way in which he entered Sweden. Changing citizenship does not mean as much to a Nordic citizen, who can move freely across Nordic borders, as it does to a refugee from, for example, Ethiopia or Uruguay. A refugee may hope to return home once the political situation has changed and, therefore, may prefer to keep his nationality.

The basic principle of Swedish nationality law is in line with the European Conventions of Limitation of Plural Citizenship. This basic principle is that dual citizenship should be avoided.

After an application for citizenship has been made to the Local Police **13.33** Board, the applicant will have to wait for about 18 months for the final decision. The Immigration Board takes at least eight of those months to progress the case. Part of this time is spent carrying out some parts of the investigation twice as the original information becomes out of date. This timescale has been highly criticised by the Swedish Parliament since it obstructs its decision to shorten the qualification time for Swedish citizenship.

Citizenship

There are four ways of acquiring Swedish citizenship: **13.34**
(i)   by birth;
(ii)   by legitimisation;
(iii) by naturalisation; or
(iv)   by registration.

Naturalisation

The Swedish Immigration Board processes some 20,000 applications for **13.35** citizenship each year, including some 500 from other Nordic countries. A boom in the number of applications is expected due to recent immigration waves.

About 85% of applications are sanctioned and 2,000 are refused due to lack of time, residence or misconduct. It is said that 30% of these are appealed to the government.

The basic rules for naturalisation of non-Nordic citizens are that the **13.36** applicant must:
(i)   have attained the age of 18;
(ii)   been domiciled in Sweden with a valid permit for the past five years; and
(iii) be of good character.

A non-Nordic national who is married to a Swedish citizen must have been resident in Sweden for three years and have been married for two years before he can obtain naturalisation. A citizen of one of the other Nordic countries must have been resident in Sweden for two years.

Domiciled is defined as: "permanent living with intention to stay". **13.37** "Intention to stay" is implied by the application for a residence permit which is, in turn, defined as the date from which residence starts. If a residence permit is issued after an illegal entry, the period of residence starts from the date when the decision was made to grant the permit. An interruption of domicile of under 30 days or, for example for military service, is not deducted. The determining factor for a break in residence is the intention to emigrate.

A crime leading to expulsion also breaks the domicile, but if it is impossible to carry out the expulsion, then domicile is calculated from the first day of the residence permit. If a legally binding deportation order is made, but again is impossible to carry out, then domicile is calculated from the date of the annulment of the deportation order.

13.38　　An investigation of good conduct is carried out by the local police board. Criminal action, debt to the state for alimony or taxes can disqualify the applicant. If, however, the applicant is physically unable to fulfil his duties then the matter may be disregarded, but if he is merely unwilling then this may be taken into consideration.

13.39　　The following terms of punishment for criminal behaviour result in a delay before the applicant can become a naturalised citizen. The fines are on a scale from 30 to 150 depending on the severity of the crime and the amount from 30 SK to 100 SEK depending on income (giving a maximum of 150,000 SEK).

Punishment		*Delay*
Fines (determined on the basis of the defendants income):		
	60 and not less than 80	1 year
	more than 80	$1\frac{1}{2}$ years
Imprisonment:	14 days	2 years
	up to 8 months	4 years
	up to 18 months	more than 4 years
	suspended sentence and probation	2 years

Repeated criminal behaviour will result in a much longer waiting period and a criminal sentence served in a foreign country is also taken into account.

13.40　　Applicants must prove that they have lost their previous citizenship within two years. Exemption is, however, awarded to political refugees and persons who are not able to renounce their first nationality. This is also the case where an application to renounce citizenship is not answered within a reasonable time. In these cases, Sweden accepts dual nationality.

From 1 January 1987 the fee for the Certificate of Citizenship is 400 SEK (80 US$). Since 1979 it has not been necessary for the applicant to have any knowledge of the Swedish language or to pass any examinations.

5. Sanctions

13.41　　A foreigner who resides in Sweden without a residence permit or one who takes up employment or works in some capacity without a work permit is subject to a fine. A Swedish citizen employing an alien who is illegally living in Sweden runs the risk of imprisonment for up to one year.

An alien or refugee giving false information to the Immigration Board can be imprisoned for up to six months. This is also the case for a person helping a foreigner to enter Sweden illegally. A person trying to hide a foreigner who is then deported from Sweden can be sentenced to imprisonment for up to one year. Organised smuggling of aliens who do not hold a residence permit into Sweden can be punished by imprisonment for up to two years.

6. Taxation considerations

A foreigner who plans to work in Sweden for several years or for an indefinite period of time must normally be considered as a resident for tax purposes. Sweden has entered into bi-lateral agreements to avoid double taxation with most countries. The Swedish level of income tax until the Swedish tax reform of 1991 was the highest in the world.

13.42

Employment income and business income (earned income derived by an individual) is taxed progressively. For 1991 the following approximate tax rates apply:

13.43

(i)   Where taxable income (assessed income reduced by a standard deduction) does not exceed SEK 170,000, the individual is liable only to municipal income tax at an average rate of approximately 31% (this varies according to the municipality). In 1991 approximately 83% of taxpayers having earned income were liable only to municipal tax on such income. For a taxable income exceeding SEK 170,000, there is an additional state tax of 20% which gives an overall marginal tax rate of approximately 51%.

(ii)   The new system for taxation of capital income represents one of the major novelties in the tax reform. For different reasons, the taxation of such income has been separated from the taxation of other income. Nominal capital income is taxed at a flat rate of 30%.

One of the most significant changes in the capital income tax is that the tax rate of 30% is applied on essentially all nominal capital gains.

The corporate income tax has been lowered to 30% and the tax base has been broadened through the abolition of most reserve options. In addition, the tax base has also been broadened through a fully nominal taxation of capital gains on shares and real estate.

In principle, corporate income is taxed twice: once at the corporate level through corporation tax and once at the shareholder level through the tax on dividends. A deduction corresponding to the value of new issued shares is being allowed as part of the tax reform. This deduction is limited to dividends distributed on new issued shares at a maximum of 10% per year of the value of the new shares, for a maximum period of 20 years. In principle, only dividends distributed to shareholders liable to tax in Sweden are deductible, for example shareholders resident in Sweden and non-residents and corporations liable to withholding tax.

The abolition of this double taxation effect and a lowering of corporate income tax to 25% is being discussed in the Swedish Parliament.

The new tax rate of 30% applies to all legal entities, corporations as well as co-operative associations, unit trusts, foundations and non-profit organisations.

13.44   The corporate income tax rate coincides with the tax rate on capital income earned by individuals and – approximately – with the social security contributions on payroll paid by corporations (28%). Thus uniformity is being improved in two dimensions, between direct and indirect household savings and between taxes on capital and employment income in the corporate sector.

Chapter 14
United Kingdom

1. Permanent immigrants

(i) Employment

(a) Employees granted work permits

Work permits are issued by the Department of Employment only where there is a clear benefit to employment and the economy of the United Kingdom, for example to ease a high level skill shortage or to enable a major new investment to take place. Work permits will only be issued for senior managers and highly skilled professionals or personnel with rare technical skills. Employers have to show that they cannot fill the vacancy with a UK or other EC national. The prospective employee should be living abroad when the employer makes the application as the Immigration Rules do not permit those admitted to the United Kingdom without work permits to switch into work permit employment. **14.1**

There are special regulations for entertainers, sports people, models and people in the hotel and catering industry. **14.2**

An application for a work permit is made in respect of a main worker required for a specific job with a specific employer. It is the employer who makes the application to the Department of Employment.

There is now in operation a two-tier system. Applications which clearly merit approval and satisfy the existing occupational skills criteria are dealt with under a simplified procedure in tier one. There are four categories of cases which fall in tier one, namely:
(i)   inter-company transfers
(ii)   board level posts with a salary of £50,000 plus per annum;
(iii)   posts involving inward investment; and
(iv)   posts where the occupation is recognised as being in short supply in the United Kingdom and European Community.

For all these employees there would be no need to advertise the post in national and local newspapers or trade journals. The requirement for an employer to advertise was necessary under the previous work permit rules in nearly all cases except for inter-company transfers.

However, advertisements in the Press will still be required for applicants in the second tier who will continue to need full documentation to demonstrate the positive benefits that will arise from the overseas workers' presence in the United Kingdom. Workers included in this category are those who are using language or cultural skills not readily available in the United Kingdom or the European Community.

[*The next paragraph is 14.5.*]

(b) Exceptions on grounds of UK ancestry

14.5 A Commonwealth citizen, one of whose grandparents was born in the United Kingdom, does not need a work permit in order to come to the United Kingdom to work. If one of his or her grandparents was born in the United Kingdom a Commonwealth citizen who wishes to take or seek employment in the United Kingdom will be granted an entry clearance for that purpose. On entry, such a person will be admitted for a period of four years whether he or she has employment or intends to look for employment.

(c) Trainees

14.6 A distinction is made between trainees and students. Trainees are those who come to the United Kingdom specifically for training or work experience and those who originally entered as visitors or students and have been allowed to change to training. It is up to the Department of Employment, and not the Home Office, to consider whether the offer of training is satisfactory.

The Department of Employment must be satisfied that the trainee intends to return abroad on completion of the training. An undertaking is usually obtained from both employer and trainee that a transfer to ordinary employment after the training period will not take place.

14.7 Special provision is made for Chartered Accountants. The Department of Employment will give approval for those who have newly qualified as Chartered Accountants to undertake employment, usually for two years, to enable them to obtain a practice certificate.

(d) Permit-free employment

14.8 Persons coming to the United Kingdom for employment in a number of specified categories such as ministers of religion, missionaries, private servants or diplomats and consuls or seamen joining ships in the United Kingdom do not need work permits. Their applications are dealt with by the Home Office rather than the Department of Employment. In all cases, permit free workers need visas prior to their entry into the United Kingdom. The initial leave will vary according to the type of employment but may not exceed 12 months, except in the case of sole representatives of overseas firms who may be admitted for an initial four-year period.

(e) Sole representatives of overseas firms

14.9 Sole representatives of overseas firms which have no branch, subsidiary or other representation in the United Kingdom will be admitted for an initial period up to four years if they hold a visa granted for that purpose. Although a visa is mandatory, one of the advantages of sole representation is that there is no obligation on the entry clearance officer to refer the case to the Home Office.

(f) Doctors and dentists

All doctors and dentists from outside the European Community are prohibited **14.10**
from entry to the United Kingdom unless they have a work permit or come
under the business rules. They used to be able to enter without a work permit
but this no longer applies.

(g) Overseas journalists and broadcasters

Representatives of overseas newspapers, news agencies and broadcasting **14.11**
organisations, on a long-term assignment to the United Kingdom, can be
admitted without having to obtain a work permit. They must, however,
obtain an entry clearance visa before arriving in the United Kingdom.

(ii) Business

(a) Businessmen and businesswomen

In order to obtain visas as businessmen or businesswomen, applicants need to **14.12**
show the following:
(i)   That they will be establishing themselves in business on their own
        account or in partnership.
(ii)   That they will be bringing money of their own to put into the business.
(iii)   That their level of financial investment will be proportional to their
        interest in the business.
(iv)   That they will be able to bear their share of the liabilities.
(v)   That they will be occupied in the running of the business.
(vi)   That there is a genuine need for their services and investment.
(vii)   That the amount of money to be invested is not less than a minimum
        amount (currently £200,000) and that this amount or more is under
        their control and disposal in the United Kingdom.
(viii) That the investment will create new, paid full-time employment for
        persons settled in the United Kingdom.
    Businessmen or women can also take over or join as partners in an existing **14.13**
business in which case they must also show the following:
(i)   A written statement of the terms on which they are to enter or take over
        the business.
(ii)   That their share of the profits will be sufficient to maintain and
        accommodate them and any dependants.
(iii)   Audited accounts of the business for the previous year.
(iv)   That the introduction of their services and investment will create new,
        paid full-time employment in the business for persons already settled in
        the United Kingdom.
(v)   That the proposed partnership or directorship is not disguised employ-
        ment.
(vi)   That they will not have to supplement their business activities by
        employment of any kind or by recourse to public funds.
    Businessmen and women will usually be admitted for an initial period of 12
months. A further three-year extension may be obtained if the applicant can

prove that the business is continuing, the money (£200,000) has been invested and that new employment has been created.

(iii) Persons of independent means/investors

14.14 Persons of independent means must make their applications from abroad. Persons given limited leave in some other capacity have no claim to remain as persons of independent means. Only the relatively wealthy can now retire to the United Kingdom. A minimum income (currently £20,000 per year) or minimum capital (currently £200,000) is now needed. In addition, persons of independent means must show a close connection with the United Kingdom or a need for their presence in the national interest. They must be able and willing to maintain themselves and support and accommodate any dependents indefinitely in the United Kingdom without working, with no assistance from any other persons, and without recourse to public funds. Where they satisfy these conditions they will normally be admitted for an initial period of four years with a prohibition on the taking of employment.

14.15 The capital or income does not have to be located in the United Kingdom but has to be disposable to the United Kingdom.

(iv) Family and marriage

14.16 There are three types of family admission to the United Kingdom:
  (i)   immediate family of persons on a limited leave such as students, workers, businessmen, persons of independent means, writers and artists;
  (ii) relatives coming on a permanent basis to settle in the United Kingdom with the rest of their family; and
  (iii) those who are allowed in to get married or who obtained settlement as a result of getting married.

(a) Marriage

14.17 Fiancés and fiancées must both apply for visas and satisfy the Entry Clearance Officer that:
  (i)   it is not the primary purpose of the intended marriage to obtain admission to the United Kingdom;
  (ii) the parties to the marriage intend to live together permanently as husband and wife;
  (iii) they have met;
  (iv) adequate maintenance and accommodation without recourse to public funds will be available for the applicant until the date of the marriage; and
  (v)   – after the marriage there will be adequate accommodation for the parties and their dependants without recourse to public funds in accommodation of their own or which they occupy themselves; and
        – after the marriage the parties will be able to maintain themselves and their dependants adequately without recourse to public funds.

(b) Spouses

The rules are very similar. They must satisfy the Entry Clearance Officer that: **14.18**

(i)   the marriage was not entered into primarily to obtain admission to the United Kingdom;

(ii)   each of the parties has the intention of living permanently with the other as his or her spouse;

(iii)   the parties to the marriage have met;

(iv)   there will be adequate accommodation for the parties and their dependants without recourse to public funds in accommodation of their own or which they occupy themselves; and

(v)   that the parties will be able to maintain themselves and their dependants adequately without recourse to public funds.

(c) Children

CHILDREN BORN IN THE UNITED KINGDOM

A child who remains in the United Kingdom continuously for the first 10 years   **14.19**
of his or her life can obtain registration as a British citizen. A child under 18, one of whose parents becomes settled or acquires British Nationality, will also be eligible for registration as a British citizen. Special rules apply to children born in the United Kingdom after 1 January 1983 who do not become British citizens. While they remain in the United Kingdom without leave there is no need to obtain leave to remain. Leave is granted which is consistent with that of the parents or parent. Where the parents live apart leave should be consistent with that of the parent who has the "day-to-day responsibility" of the child or children.

OTHER CHILDREN

Admission of unmarried children under the age of 18 living in conventional   **14.20**
families is unconditional. Admission of children of divided or single parent families is qualified and difficult. The burden of proof is on the applicants who want to come to the United Kingdom. They may have to prove that they are their parents' children or that the children are the ages they claim.

CHILDREN OVER 18

Children over 18 (other than fully dependent unmarried daughters under 21)   **14.21**
must qualify in their own right unless there are the most exceptional compassionate circumstances.

ADOPTED CHILDREN

Where a court in the United Kingdom makes an Adoption Order in favour of a   **14.22**
parent who is a British citizen the child will automatically become a British citizen. Adopted children are only treated as natural children for the purpose of applications to settle in the United Kingdom where there has been a genuine transfer of parental responsibility on the grounds of the original parents' inability to care for the child, and the adoption is not one of convenience

arranged to facilitate the child's admission into the United Kingdom. But there is no provision in the Immigration Rules for a child to be brought to the United Kingdom for adoption. This is a matter in the discretion of the Home Office.

(d) Parents and grandparents

14.23 It is only widowed mothers, fathers who are widowers aged 65 or over, or parents travelling together of whom at least one is aged 65 or over, who usually are given permission to join their children in the United Kingdom. The parents or grandparents must be:

(i)   wholly or mainly dependent upon,

(ii)   sons or daughters settled in the United Kingdom,

(iii) who have the means to maintain their parents and any other relatives who would be admissible as dependants of the parents, and

(iv)   have adequate accommodation for them.

14.24 They must also be without other close relatives in their own country to turn to. Where a parent has remarried there is an additional requirement. That parent should not be admitted unless he or she cannot look to the spouse or children of the second marriage for support and the children in the United Kingdom have sufficient means and accommodation to support both the parent and any spouse or children of the second marriage who would be admissible as dependants.

(e) Other relatives

14.25 The only relatives who can now qualify, apart from parents, are sons, daughters, sisters, brothers and uncles and aunts. They must be wholly or mainly dependent on their sponsor in the United Kingdom. They must be living alone and in the most exceptional compassionate circumstances.

[*The next paragraph is 14.28.*]

2. Visitors, students and temporary workers

(i) Visitors

14.28 People seeking entry as visitors must satisfy the Immigration authorities that:

> "They are genuinely seeking entry for the period of the visit as stated by them; for that period they will maintain and accommodate themselves and any dependants or will all be maintained and accommodated adequately by their relatives or friends; they will do so without working or recourse to public funds; they can meet the costs of the return or onward journey."

14.29 They must specify the length of the proposed visit. It must not exceed six months and the Immigration Officer usually gives six months on entry unless there are exceptional circumstances. Before giving admission, the Immigration Officer has to be satisfied that the person is genuinely seeking entry for the period of visit as stated by him or her and does not intend to overstay or to take employment.

People coming in as medical visitors are treated differently and more sympathetically.

(ii) Business visits

Visitors are normally prohibited from taking employment and sometimes also from entering into any business or profession. Neither form of prohibition prevents business visitors from transacting business during their visit.

14.30

(iii) Students

Persons wanting to enter the United Kingdom as overseas students must obtain a visa from a British Embassy abroad before leaving their country, even if they are not visa nationals. They must be full-time students; able to pay for their course; and intend to return home when their studies are complete. Some students will have been accepted for their courses by the time they apply for a visa or arrive in the United Kingdom. Others will merely be prospective students. Both can come, but prospective students only qualify for admission if, amongst other things, they have a genuine and realistic intention of studying.

14.31

(iv) Prospective students

Students who have not yet enrolled on a course can obtain entry clearance and admission as prospective students. They must be able to satisfy the Immigration Authorities that:

(i)　they have genuine and realistic intentions of studying in the United Kingdom;

(ii)　they can, without working and without recourse to public funds, meet the cost of their intended course and of their own maintenance and accommodation and that of any dependants during the course; and

(iii)　that they intend to leave the United Kingdom after completion of their studies.

They may then be admitted for a short period, within the limit of their means, with a prohibition on the taking of employment and will be advised to apply to the Home Office for further consideration of their case.

14.32

(v) Medical students

A person accepted for training as a nurse or midwife at a hospital should be granted a visa as a student unless there is evidence that he or she has obtained acceptance by misrepresentation or does not intend to follow the course. Nurses and midwives are allowed to accept offers of employment on completion of their training provided they are not funded by the government. Provision is also made for the admission of graduates of UK Medical Schools to undertake pre-registration House Officer employment for up to 12 months as required for full registration with the General Medical Council. Doctors and

14.33

dentists can be admitted for postgraduate training for an aggregate period of up to four years, but there must be an intention to leave at the end of the postgraduate studies.

(vi) Wives and children of students

14.34   The wife and children under 18 of a person admitted as a student are to be given leave to enter for the same period as the student if they can be maintained and accommodated without recourse to public funds. Their freedom to take employment is not to be restricted unless the student himself is prohibited from taking employment, in which case the prohibition extends to the wife and children.

(vii) Au pairs

14.35   "Au pair" is an arrangement under which an unmarried person aged 17–27 inclusive and without dependants, who is a national of a Western European country including Malta, Cyprus and Turkey may come to the United Kingdom to learn the English language and to live for a time as a member of an English speaking family. When the Immigration Officer is satisfied that an au pair arrangement has been made, the au pair may be admitted for a period of up to 12 months with a prohibition on taking employment. If he or she has previously spent time in the United Kingdom as an au pair she may be admitted for a further period provided that the total aggregate period in which he or she will be in the United Kingdom does not exceed two years. There is nothing to stop a person in the United Kingdom as a visitor or in some other temporary capacity switching to "au pair".

(viii) Working holidaymakers

14.36   Young British Commonwealth citizens aged 17–27 are entitled to admission to the United Kingdom for up to two years as working holidaymakers if they satisfy the Immigration Officer that they are coming to the United Kingdom for an extended holiday before settling down in their own country, and that they intend to take only employment which will be incidental to their holiday. Some financial backing is required and the rules provide that working holidaymakers must have the means to pay for their return journey and will not need to have recourse to public funds.

3. Refugees and political asylum

14.37   There may be many reasons for seeking political asylum, but persons are only refugees within the meaning of the Convention Relating to the Status of Refugees and the Protocol to the Convention if they seek to escape persecution for reasons of race, religion, nationality, membership of a social group, or political opinion. In the United Kingdom all those who are granted political asylum are recognised as Convention Refugees and given appropriate documents. Special considerations apply where a person claims asylum in the United Kingdom where it appears that he or she might be eligible for asylum as a result of anything the person has said. All such cases are referred to the Home Office regardless of any other grounds of refusal under the Rules. Once the cases go to the Home Office they will be considered in accordance with the Convention and Protocol. Where the Home Office grants asylum the Immigration Officer will grant leave to enter. If asylum is refused, then the Immigration Officer will consider whether the person is entitled to remain on some other basis under the Immigration Rules. Asylum claims made after entry are usually considered by the Home Office's Refugee Unit.

In some cases where the Home Office considers that the persons do not have **14.38** an entitlement to political asylum they give leave to remain on an exceptional basis. It is called "exceptional leave" because it is given outside the Immigration Rules. It is not a recognition of refugee status and holders of such exceptional leave who consider that they ought to have refugee status are given the right to appeal against the refusal to grant political asylum.

4. Permanent residence and nationality

(i) Permanent residence

In order to apply for permanent residence or settlement a person, together **14.39** with his or her spouse and children admitted as his or her dependants, must have legally resided for four years in any one of the immigration categories which includes the category of refugee.

(ii) Nationality

One year after permanent residence (*i.e.* five years after entry and normally **14.40** eight years after entry in the case of an asylum seeker being granted exceptional leave to remain) the applicant can apply for naturalisation as a British citizen. To qualify, he or she must not have spent more than 450 days outside the United Kingdom throughout the five-year period and not more than 90 days in the last year prior to making the application.

However, the spouse of a British citizen may apply for naturalisation one year after permanent residence (*i.e.* three years after entry) and to qualify he or she must not have spent more than 270 days outside the United Kingdom throughout the three-year period and not more than 90 days in the last year prior to making the application.

(iii) **Immigration categories leading to permanent residence**

14.41 A person admitted into the United Kingdom in any of the following categories may, if he or she so qualifies, apply for permanent residence:

(i)   approved employment;

(ii)   permit free employment (*i.e.* sole representatives of overseas firms, ministers of religion, missionaries, representatives of overseas newspapers and broadcasters, employees of overseas governments or the United Nations or other international body and operational ground staff (but not other staff) of overseas-owned airlines;

(iii)   businessmen and women who have set up business with others;

(iv)   self-employed businessmen and women;

(v)   writers or artists;

(vi)   persons of independent means;

(vii)   workers or work-seekers who are Commonwealth citizens and whose grandparents were born in the United Kingdom.

5. **Home Office discretion**

14.42 It cannot be emphasised enough that the Home Office has very considerable discretion to waive or vary most of the requirements referred to in this chapter. The individual circumstances of each applicant are taken into account. The exercise of ministerial discretion outside the Immigration Rules is an important aspect of immigration law and practice in the United Kingdom.

6. **Sanctions**

(i) **Deportation**

14.43 Any person who is a non-British citizen is liable to deportation on the grounds:

(i)   He or she does not comply with any condition of leave, for example, by overstaying his or her leave or working in breach of condition.

(ii)   The Home Secretary deems his or her deportation to be conducive to the public good.

(iii)   In some cases where another member of the family, such as the father or mother is to be deported.

(iv)   Where a court recommends deportation after a conviction for an offence punishable by imprisonment.

(ii) **Illegal entry**

14.44 To become an illegal entrant a person must unlawfully enter or seek to enter the United Kingdom in breach of a Deportation Order or the Immigration Laws. There are five kinds of possible illegal entry:

(i)   entry without leave;

(ii)　entry in breach of a Deportation Order;
(iii)　seamen who desert ship and overstay;
(iv)　entry through the Common Travel Area;
(v)　entry by deception.

(iii) Detention

Immigration Officers are authorised to detain the following categories of **14.45**
person:
(i)　Persons arriving by ship or aircraft in the United Kingdom may be
　　detained pending their examination by an Immigration Officer to see
　　whether they need or should be granted leave to enter.
(ii)　Those refused leave to enter may be detained pending their removal
　　from the United Kingdom.
(iii)　Illegal entrants may be detained pending their removal if they are not
　　given leave to enter or remain in the United Kingdom.
(iv)　Members of the crew of a ship or aircraft who stay longer than
　　permitted, or are reasonably suspected of intending to do so by an
　　Immigration Officer, may be detained pending their removal.

(iv) Detention by the Home Secretary

In addition to the powers of detention by Immigration Officers, the Home **14.46**
Secretary has wide powers to detain persons liable to deportation. This may
occur in three situations:
(i)　after a court recommendation;
(ii)　where notice has been given to a person of a decision to make a
　　Deportation Order; or
(iii)　where a Deportation Order is in force against any person, he or she may
　　be detained under the authority of the Home Secretary and pending his
　　or her removal or departure from the United Kingdom.

7. Tax and social benefit considerations

These are very complex in the United Kingdom and are, therefore, beyond the **14.47**
scope of this chapter.

Index